Brave

Brave

COURAGEOUSLY LIVE YOUR TRUTH

SHEILA VIJEYARASA

ROCKPOOL

For my nieces and nephews:
may you spread your wings and fly
as far as you want, and in any direction you wish,
feeling free and full of possibilities.

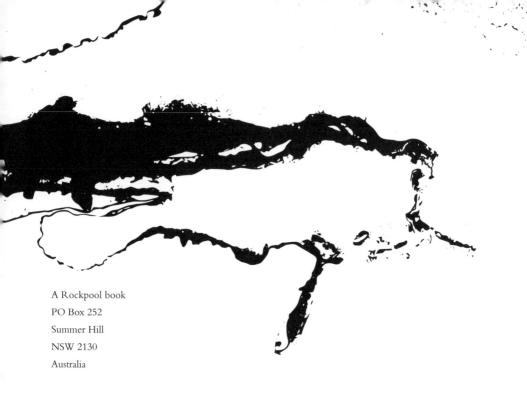

A Rockpool book
PO Box 252
Summer Hill
NSW 2130
Australia

rockpoolpublishing.co
Follow us! **f** **◎** rockpoolpublishing
Tag your images with #rockpoolpublishing

ISBN: 9781925946406

Published in 2021 by Rockpool Publishing
Copyright text © Sheila Vijeyarasa 2021
Copyright photos © Paul Robbins 2021
Copyright design © Pockpool Publishing 2021

Design and typesetting by Sara Lindberg, Rockpool Publishing

NATIONAL
LIBRARY
OF AUSTRALIA

A catalogue record for this
book is available from the
National Library of Australia

Printed and bound in China
10 9 8 7 6 5 4 3 2

Contents

Brave is a must read for anyone who wants to overcome their fears so they can fulfil their destiny. Sheila's voice has profound wisdom, wisdom that is based on a lifetime of achieving tremendous success in multiple realities. Sheila is a wise guide who will inspire and encourage you to walk your own Courageous Path. Her powerful lessons combined with the voices of many others provide a rich diversity of experiences and stories from meaningful people who only do work with meaning. Brave is an important read for anyone who is feeling lost, inspiring us all to step into our lives in the most powerful way.

PAULINE NGUYEN, AWARD-WINNING AUTHOR, INTERNATIONAL SPEAKER, SPIRITUAL ENTREPRENEUR

For the woman caught between two worlds, this book is for you. Pulling together concepts of healing and bravery with a modern twist, you'll be bathed in wisdom and practicality as Sheila's words present truths we've suppressed and courage we haven't yet tapped into.

TAMMI KIRKNESS, AUTHOR OF THE PANIC BUTTON BOOK

Sheila is the kind of woman you meet and who you would seriously consider to be an echo of an ancient goddess from long ago. Her open heart genuinely lives in a balance of empowerment and vulnerability, and she has an uncanny ability to transcend the norm and reflect real wisdom from the ether above. Hers is a story of our own and it manages to find a way to crack light into the heart. Brave is ultimately a no-nonsense hand guide to living with collective, universal magic, to breathing creative fire into the lungs and reclaiming the seat of power from within your soul's core. I could not put this book down.

ANDRÉS ENGRACIA, AUTHOR OF PURE MAGIC ORACLE

Brave *is a must read for these current times. It inspires us all to embrace life and realise our potential. Sheila's wisdom has the power to not only validate the struggles of women, but to heal and provide a roadmap in the awakening process.*

TOM CRONIN, COACH, MEDITATION TEACHER AND PRODUCER OF THE PORTAL (FILM AND BOOK)

Brave *is a powerfully insightful and heartfelt book that honours the collective insights of many profound and wise women. If you are a woman ready to embrace her feminine power, Sheila is a wise guide who will inspire and encourage you to walk your own path.* Brave *inspires us all to step into our lives in a powerful way. Sheila's wisdom, earned from her extensive studies and the highs and lows of her lived experience, has the power to not only validate the struggles of women, but also to heal and provide guidance. This is an important book for anyone who wants to face their fears, fulfill their destiny and find a meaningful way forward. There is a great deal of wisdom in Sheila's powerful lessons combined with the voices of many other women. If you are looking for the next step on your own journey, 'Brave' could show the way.*

MARGOT SAVILLE, AUTHOR OF THE BATTLE FOR BENNELONG AND CRIKEY.COM.AU JOURNALIST

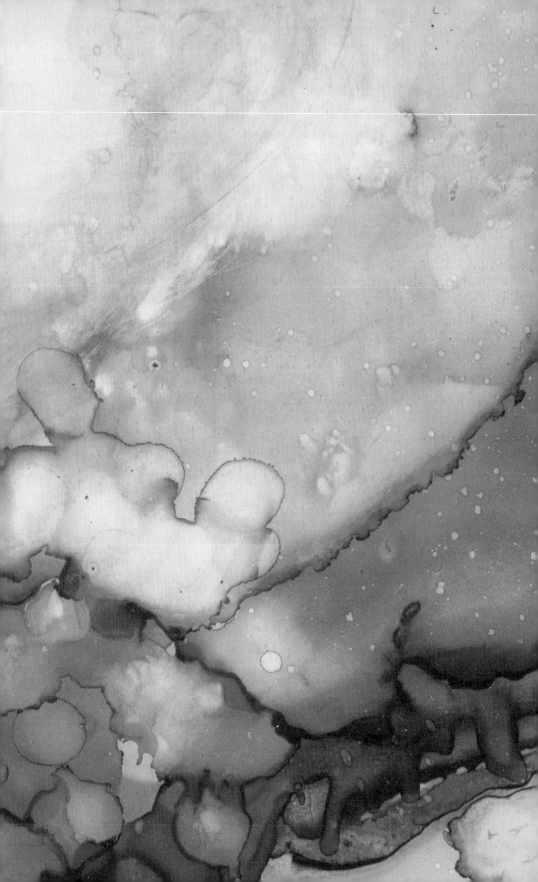

An invitation to walk the Courageous Path

We become addicted to the life we don't even like.
– JOE DISPENZA

Welcome to the Courageous Path. Your Courageous Path: the path to becoming authentically you. There can be a huge chasm between a desire to live an authentic life and truly living an authentic life. The gap between the two is bravery. You have always had bravery; it has just become a little lost within you, and when fear gets in the way you forget.

Being me and being you should be the simplest thing in the world. But as you already know, it's not that easy! Through my own experiences I have come to realise it is an act of courage to be true and authentic to myself. My acts of courage were a mixture of small and large actions, some not big enough to make it to my social media news feed. It will be the same for you: you must be courageous enough to answer the call to be yourself.

The call is a yearning for change. Within each of us we can hear it and we can feel it, yet we still get confused as to how to make sustainable changes happen in our lives.

You may feel a longing, knowing there is more than what you currently have. You may be new to the idea of a spiritual path, embarking on a cycle of personal growth or reaching for new teachings and insights. You may feel you have no idea where you are, that you are a little lost. You may be at a fork in the road.

One road is more of the same version of your life: the safe, predictable and lacklustre path full of the same worries and concerns. It is highly probable this is someone else's path you are walking on. The other road presents more of an unknown; fear and a lack of courage prevent you from taking the other path. Until you allow the real you to show up on these journeys it is not your journey, and this path will most certainly lead you to familiar disappointment. My intuition tells me you desire a great adventure, that you desire liberation and are seeking to return home: to find yourself, your true self. This is what the other path promises. It is the less travelled path. The path for the brave. The Courageous Path.

Wherever you are right now you are in the perfect place. The universe has brought you here'. Of this I am certain.

This book is an instruction manual, companion and guidebook to help *you* to step into a courageous life: your very own unapologetic version of you. I have used much of what I went through on my own path to create the steps in this book. Before my Courageous Path I was a walking juxtaposition of uber confidence and self-doubt, of over-conviction and uncertainty, of pride and self-loathing. What a party of one! Then I had a massive 'hell, yeah' moment and thought: 'Is it more important to fit in, or get courageous and curious enough to do me?' I finally found the courageous me waiting to be seen, listened to and acknowledged. This didn't happen just once; it was a continuous calling to answer the question. Responding to the calling is what courage is.

My path called me to quit my big seductive job as a finance director at a prestigious publishing house. It called me to honour my spiritual path to become a spiritual teacher and intuitive medium, a bridge between the spirit world and the physical world. Crazy, right? I loved my job. But I loved myself more and I knew I had a calling, a dharma, a life purpose: this big lumpy *something* I needed to do. I felt a call to connect with spirit guides and higher beings, to bring through transformative and insightful information, to help others powerfully move forward on their Courageous Paths.

I also found courage in love. I had sublimated and sacrificed myself for too many others. I had a guru I was loyal to, a shaman I was devoted to; I worshipped the corporate gods and loved myself too little. I dug deep and uncovered the sassy, single, brave woman – a goddess – who would only accept the highest form of love. I didn't settle down, I settled up. I stepped into my courageous life, in a way that made sense to no one but myself.

Baby steps, big steps and giant leaps: they are all part of the path leading towards authenticity. Finding the courageous woman within you is your most heroic quest. *She* does exist.

In the following pages you will read the stories of women who are following their Courageous Paths. They are women like you and me who have found their own unique flavour of extraordinary. Their stories are inspirational blueprints, so allow them to be a mirror for you to view your own truths and access your own courage and wisdom.

I have included a toolkit that will ensure the changes you make in your life are enduring and transformative as you bravely travel the Courageous Path.

THE TOOLKIT

- Courageous truths: these are the truths that will help you move beyond your current status quo. Your inner compass will know that these are the points to follow.

- Get curious questions: these questions create a truthful inner reflection, so don't underestimate the value in answering them. There is wisdom within you that wishes to speak through the pages of your journal.

- Be still practices: these are meditation or breathing practices that will support you on your Courageous Path. These practices aim to help you to stop and listen to your inner voice.

- Power phrases: a mantra or affirmation can bring focus and calm within your mind. The more powerful your thoughts the more powerful your life. These mantras help to create changes in your thinking and mindset.

The fact that you are here is evidence you have listened to your inner guidance and are willing to reclaim the courageous part of you that has been cast adrift. I honour you for showing up to do this brave work.

Let's journey together. It is time to be courageously you.

With love, Sheila.

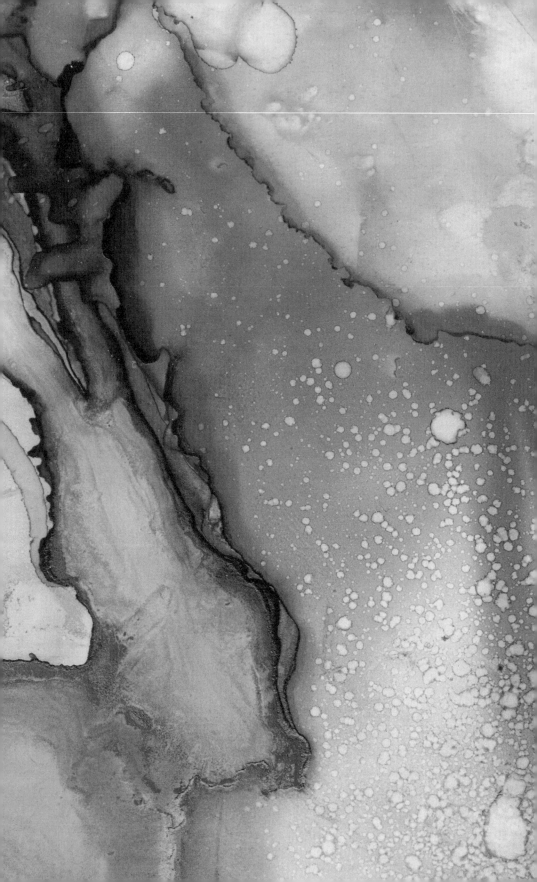

CHAPTER 1

Bravely waking up

> You can lose your job but you
> can't lose your calling.
>
> **– MARIANNE WILLIAMSON**

FIFTY SHADES OF PAIN

Sometimes we don't even know that we are lost. Or in pain. Or struggling to be our authentic selves. We can spend weeks, months and years pretending that our life is okay, perhaps even okay. Then we come to a decisive moment when we realise: this isn't working anymore. I had this moment in my mid–30s and realised I was not where I wanted to be.

Do you know this place? Have you been there? Are you there now?

Let me rewind to a few months before that moment. I was in a publishing meeting when an executive turned to me and said: 'Have you read this *Fifty* book? *Fifty* something . . . *Fifty Shades?* I think we have something here!'

I was head of the finance analytical team at Random House, single and relatively young. One hundred and twenty million people had yet to devour the sacred text *Fifty Shades of Grey*; we felt we were on the cusp of something big.

It is commonplace for new manuscripts to be circulated *ad nauseam* in a publishing house, but there was something different this time: I felt *called* to read this manuscript. When something big is about to erupt you feel the energy tug you in, even if you don't know why. This is what a *calling* feels like: there is a magnetic pull you can't ignore and there is a knowing that the world, your world, is about to change forever.

Later that afternoon I sat in my office – wide-eyed, red-faced and sweaty – and swallowed up the manuscript. Spiritual souls, please do not judge! My intuition was telling me we had something big; the time was right, it was a book that spoke to women and there was a collective calling for it. But at that point none of us really knew what we had on our hands: a runaway bestseller.

In book publishing land, when a bestseller comes our way we all gather in sacred circles, face the east, burn incense and pay homage to the author who has given us these temporary riches. It is a super blue moon, rare and to be honoured.

As an analyst it was a relief to report this phenomenon. At work, the months that followed were marked by champagne corks popping, revenue line graphs all pointing up and staggering market share growth. Any woman who works in finance understands that our monthly cycle and emotions are tied less to the lunar phases and more to the month-end accounting cycle. A great profit result meant a couple of pain-free weeks and an inner calm. No Ibuprofen needed.

Buddhist noble truth: nothing is permanent.

At the time I was in the middle of a distinction-laden MBA. I had a job title I had worked hard to earn. Behind closed doors my life was fifty shades of anxiety. My mind and spirit were restless. I was living a life I was not comfortable with and I was asleep to the truth as to why. How could everything at work appear so exciting yet I felt numb to it all? I had worked so hard to get here, isn't this what I should want? I felt a mounting pressure to keep performing despite feeling it would be at the expense of who I really was. I was frustrated because I had created a life that didn't stir and excite me.

I was in the middle of my 'successful' life, suddenly realising it was not where I wanted to be. I was lost, yet I did not realise how lost I was. I was in pain, yet I had become numb to the daily emotional pain I was in. I had worked hard to create what I thought was a meaningful career, yet other aspects of my life felt empty and lacking in connection. My inner compass was broken and I was left with no sense of direction. I was a contradiction: in the corporate world I was a leader, yet I was not a leader in my private life. I was a workaholic.

When you indulge in workaholism you put others in charge of your life while you focus on tasks, projects and replying to emails that have very little to do with your calling or your purpose. When you are a workaholic you neglect to open your heart to deep love. Dating felt like another task on my to-do list. You stop being generous with your time with family and friends, and when you do spend time with them you are not present. Your world starts to get smaller and smaller even while your corporate career or professional life appears to get bigger and bigger.

Fortunately for me the universe decided that this flavour of success was not meant to last.

There are a million ways to be asleep to your truth. Working long exhausting hours is just one way.

THE PAIN OF PRESSURE

Perfectionism is self-abuse of the highest order.
ANNE WILSON SCHAEF

People pleaser and under pressure to be more: aren't all women *fifty shades* of these ways of being, depending on our astrology, moonology and biology?

Striving to be more is exhausting and keeps us busy, very busy. It shows up as impossible goals, standards beyond reason and self-worth tied entirely to productivity, accomplishment and looking good. In more extreme scenarios we can be considered a perfectionist. Perfectionists are irrational and obsessive and forget there is a bigger picture. When perfectionists say they seek the truth often what they really seek is validation, and no amount of external validation will ever feed their hungry soul. There is no positive feedback loop.

When I was 12 years old I first met my perfectionist self. I was close to being demoted to 'the B class', a class that I thought, in my 12-year-old mind, was for the second bests. I came from a super high-performing family, which didn't need to be a problem, but my self-worth was so low it started to become a major one.

I was on the cusp of adolescence and had a complete inability to manage my emotional states. When love does not come from within we seek it from anyone and anything. The seeking of it is a relentless and exhausting pursuit.

My perfectionism had a devastating effect on my self-esteem and I suffered my first bout of crippling depression and anxiety. The thing with perfectionism is that you are never good enough – ever. While failing does not need to be an issue, when you are a perfectionist the shame of failing can be debilitating. The shame of not being good enough, being average or even making a small mistake takes you out of the game of life quickly and you create a life that ensures you never fail.

Can you imagine how utterly exhausting that is?

At the age of 12 I went looking for love and acceptance by studying like I was trying to get into Harvard Law, except I was in the sixth grade. I studied morning, noon and night. I ate meals at my study desk. I was committed to not being in 'the B class'. Then something happened at the end of sixth grade: I topped the class. After nearly flunking I came first in the year. Crazy, eh? Everyone thought it was because I was smart, but I just worked hard that year. Damn hard.

The validation that came with the label 'dux' was incredibly gratifying, but what appeared to be a great outcome externally actually became a big problem in that it set up a horrid pattern for my adult life: the need to be perfect, to never fail.

This is how patterns in life start: with a need to survive or to hunt for love, acceptance and approval. We find a way to get it, and for me it was being successful. Then we copy and paste that pattern every day, week and month. I spent the next thirty years running from 'the B class'. Eventually we have a nervous breakdown – for me it was several.

The need to be perfect means that average or even anything less than perfect feels like a failure. It means you seek out where things are not right and then you make yourself wrong. People pleasers are no different. Our thoughts betray us: we stop believing we have a natural intelligence, believing instead that we are stupid and need to work harder than everyone else to succeed and for people to like us. We may believe we are ugly, yet we get compliments about our appearance. We may believe we are overweight, when in reality we are healthy. We may believe we aren't good enough and are more focused on how it should be rather accepting how it is. It means life feels like one hard slog.

In his research paper 'Perfectionism and Acceptance' Lars-Gunnar Lundh said: 'There is nothing unhealthy or dysfunctional about the striving for perfection as such – perfectionism, however, becomes dysfunctional when this striving for perfection turns into a demand for perfection, defined as an inability to accept being less than perfect.' During my corporate career I demanded perfection from myself. Success was not an *option*; it was *critical* for my survival.

There is a much greater cost that is necessary to talk about. When you are a perfectionist and a people pleaser you don't dare take on your life purpose, as the risk of failing is too great and the needs of others are more important than your own. Instead of pursuing my purpose I found meaning in monotonous spreadsheets and double-entry bookkeeping.

Is your perfectionism and people pleasing exhausting you?

FIFTY SHADES OF FAILURE

When you are at war with yourself and you win, who loses?
CARL BUCHHEIT

When life decides it has had enough of our perfectionism and our need to please others it conspires to free us from it by letting us fail. Alongside a small group of executives, I was responsible for forecasting book sales and predicting how much stock to order. I was sitting in my office staring at a metaphorical dartboard, my forecasting tool of choice for a runaway bestseller. Having consulted my peers, I signed off on another shipment of *Fifty Shades of Grey*; the books would arrive six weeks later. This book seemed unstoppable, averaging one sale per second globally while elsewhere there were cracks showing in the industry. One major bookstore retailer had gone bust, and the arrival of ebooks was threatening the stability of the institution that was publishing.

And then it happened: a week later, sales stopped.

Dead.

I had not only missed the bull's eye, I had missed the entire dartboard.

On the day this happened I wished that both myself and the cargo ship transporting the substantial reprint of *Fifty Shades of Grey* to Sydney would sink into the abyss of the sea.

The thing is, *we* got it wrong but *I* took it personally. Even though it was a shared failure, I experienced the failure as my failure alone. Getting a stock forecast wrong in publishing is not an uncommon phenomenon, but some failures feel bigger than others. I had taken on the emotional burdens of my company. Women do that; we make ourselves emotional beasts regardless of our title or titles: mother, entrepreneur, wife, girlfriend, CEO. And when looking out for everybody else we don't get time to look inwards at our own lives.

The world was celebrating this successful bestseller and I was looking up to the corporate gods – my bosses – desperately trying to explain the unexplainable error. No one could have predicted this.

Upon reflection a small part of me was relieved to fail. When we are perfectionists, failure is a reprieve from the highly anxious state, the rat race, the treadmill. It is the red card that takes us off the field so we can collapse and catch our breath. We can watch the game that continues to be played and start to think: 'This is not working. How does the game plan need to change?'

It is a similar story for people pleasers: we don't always get it right and we can't always make people happy. When we don't get the positive reinforcement, the validation that we are liked, it too can feel like a failure.

Life will teach you that the only way to overcome perfectionism and people pleasing is to fail. To let the disintegrating marriage, the job redundancy, the bankruptcy, bring you to your knees. To let the failure teach you that it is okay to fail.

The biggest lesson we need to learn is that love is always present. Our actions, achievements, goals and medals of a blockbuster life do not make us more worthy or lovable. Sometimes that realisation can only come in the muddy trenches of life. And being truly free from the pressure to be something we are not is the freedom to be ourselves. This was the freedom I was seeking.

Can you see your failures as a teacher?

WAKING UP TO THE WAKE-UP CALL

To see your drama is to be liberated from it.

KEN KEYES JR

Failure can wake us up. Sometimes we need a spotlight shone directly into our eyes. For me, *Fifty Shades of Grey* was that spotlight.

My mind, body and soul were perpetually exhausted. When I looked into the mirror I was not the fairest of them all; I was apathetic and restless. Depression wasn't constant because it was kept at bay when I was busy. So what did I do? I became an expert at busy. A part of me wanted to awaken, but a larger part of me wanted to remain asleep to my truth.

> *Tired women do not wake up to their purpose.*

Spiritual teacher Eckhart Tolle describes in *The Power of Now*: 'If you are trapped in a nightmare you will be strongly motivated to awaken than someone who is just caught in the ups and downs of an ordinary dream.'

I plummeted into a depression and felt the *Fifty Shades of Failure*. The failure wasn't just quarantined to my job and a single incorrect stock forecast: nothing felt right in my life any more. Alone in the world, I was now forced to slow down so I could understand what had gone wrong. Examining, exploring and thinking clearly about what mattered to me in my life was the work I was *called* to do. I became aware that my purpose had not yet shown up in life because *I* had not shown up in life.

For many of us, dissatisfaction with our jobs is common because it is rarely where our purpose resides or where our true gifts and passions are expressed. At some point we must begin the transition away from this safe destination.

During the depth of my depression I started to identify my struggle. I was moving into a phase of some awareness and yet all I felt was confusion; acceptance and clarity would come later. I wanted immediate clarity as to my purpose and the correct next steps – an instruction manual for the way forward. My intuition was telling me that purpose wasn't a single event or a destination. I was starting to realise that the next steps would be potentially uncomfortable.

I also knew I had to stop wearing exhaustion as a badge of honour. At work I convinced myself that something would go wrong if I didn't do everything myself. I needed to surrender my controlling nature and learn how to trust. I needed to ask for help and to see this as a strength and not a weakness.

I also had to look at my unresolved emotional issues and take responsibility as to why I was not attracting available love into my life. I was either anxious in love or running away from commitment, and trying to find 'the one' was a constant central drama in my life. Dating felt like a hunt and not a fun and exciting game; it was hard work and no play.

Overcoming perfectionism can feel truly impossible at times. Workaholism – an expression of perfectionism – is the only addiction that you are rewarded for. As a perfectionist you get a lot of positive feedback: you receive validation, job promotions and sparkly new titles. There is zero motivation to overcome a way of being that society places a great value on. I was, however, starting to become aware that the costs of my perfectionism were now outweighing the benefits. This realisation created a possibility for change.

At this point I was called to step onto my Courageous Path. I was not aware that I was being turned into the heroine of my own life; only hindsight would reveal this. I felt utterly lost and like a failure in many aspects of my life. I wanted to hide, but instead I summoned up the courage and started to walk forward on my path.

Awakening cannot be undone.

HEAD OVER HEART

The things you are passionate about are not random, they are your calling.
FABIENNE FREDRICKSON

Sometimes the answers to our big questions are in our past.

Let me press rewind.

When I was 21 I found myself in a second-hand bookstore holding a deck of tarot cards and wondering why. Why was I drawn to these beautiful, mystical cards?

Why was I at the back of the store in secrecy? Why was I conflicted so much of the time?

For me that conflict was between my world-facing persona (high achiever, people pleaser) and my inner truth (the woman drawn to the spiritual, the woman certain there was more going on beneath the surface). I still remember the way my pulse sped up when I pulled that first card from the tarot deck. I felt confusion rushing through me. I could sense it would change my life if I let it and I could sense that the cost would be great. My inner truth was that I didn't know if I wanted to climb the ladder that followed the traditional cultural path of marriage and family, the ambitious corporate ladder or another ladder altogether.

My logical left brain kicked in. I carefully placed the card back in the deck and sighed. I was an accountant on the journey to becoming a CFO yet my heart was aching for the mystical. 'Heart, you can wait,' I thought. 'The mind has a lot of work to do. The mind has to become a chartered accountant, do an MBA, climb that beautiful corporate ladder and make it to the top.'

I was so disconnected from my real values and my truthful self that, much like in the game of snakes and ladders, my goal was to keep climbing any ladder as long as I got higher. The types of ladders did not matter; I thought it was avoiding the snakes that counted. In dream analysis snakes represent our fears and quite often our fears are not real.

I put the tarot deck back on the shelf and grabbed a copy of Richard Branson's newly published business biography, *Losing My Virginity*. I decided I wanted to climb corporate Everest, even though I was creating a life that was not in alignment with my values.

Inner conflict kept building and was forming into an avalanche. I still kept on climbing. It would be many more years before the avalanche would engulf me and return me to the place where I would hold a deck of tarot cards, a place where I would step onto my spiritual path professionally as a teacher, medium and healer.

There is a great height to fall from when you climb up ladders that are not yours to climb.

BETRAYAL OF OUR INTUITION

This is our third women's revolution.

ARIANNA HUFFINGTON

Not so long ago, when a woman actively followed her intuition she was rounded up and burned at the stake. It sort of makes sense that we're scared of that little voice inside our heart, but here's the uncomfortable truth I've discovered: no matter how hard we try to ignore it, that seemingly tiny little voice *is* the voice of our soul, of our truth. That voice is here to stay and it will become louder. That voice longs to be heard; in fact, she wants to roar.

In 1252 Pope Innocent IV (oh, the irony) was terrified of women and their innate ability to heal, birth, nurture, know, see things and ultimately lead. For the next five and a half centuries millions of women were persecuted because of their instinctive and truthful voices. Women were lined up and led off. The authorities came for the healers first, then the women who walked with conviction, independence and knowledge. Still too feminine, too wise. Finally, the older women with the real wisdom were rounded up. They were natural seers, the real leaders, comfortable in their own skin. They were not scared of power and especially not their own. They were those in authority and were feared the most. They were our great grandmothers, great-great grandmothers and beyond. We do not know many of their stories as their stories were burned with their bodies.

Forget who once burned us. We no longer need to burn ourselves out.

Not listening to our intuition is the greatest war we can wage on ourselves.

In *Thrive*, Arianna Huffington describes several revolutions that have marked the feminine uprising. The first revolution, led by the suffragettes in the 1880s, fought for basic equality. The second revolution led by Gloria Steinem and Betty Friedan in the 1970s expanded the roles of women in society. The current revolution is one that deals with our own individual courage honouring our intuition and life path.

In that *Fifty Shades* time I valued my intellect over my intuition and emotions. I was busy doing, not feeling. I saw meditation, mindfulness and simply stopping to take a break as lazy, wasteful and indulgent. Even if I wanted to stop I didn't have the tools or the skills to do so. No one had taught me how to stop. There was no masters in mindfulness and meditation or bachelor degree in intuitive studies. I was becoming aware there was a conflict within myself, that my inner voice wanted to be heard. I was being called to listen.

When we deny our intuition, the side effects are fear and inner conflict.

BLACK SHEEP SYNDROME

No one can make you feel inferior without your consent.

ELEANOR ROOSEVELT

I belonged to a culture where you don't freeze your eggs and delay your fertility plans; you curry your eggs loyally for your husband. I took on these expectations as my own truth and felt the pressure to keep up with my girlfriends as they moved elegantly into their roles as wives and mothers. I felt my culture did not acknowledge or recognise me for who I was and, worse, I did not acknowledge myself for who I was. When we feel like an outcast or that we don't fit in, we are in fact projecting the part of ourselves *we* have cast out.

'I am the black sheep of the family,' I said once to my cousin. She and I were the only two unmarried and childless women in our large Sri Lankan–Australian family. I was taken aback by the shock on her face.

'No way!' she challenged me. 'And no one has ever called you the black sheep. You called yourself that.'

The penny dropped. I *had* called myself that.

In that moment I realised that I was not the black sheep; I was not even a sheep. I was actually a wolf: fearless and a leader in my life. Wolves have had a bad reputation historically; fairy tales have taught us they are dangerous. We don't want to be the big bad wolf. These were the stories I needed to untell myself.

Married, unmarried, the lady boss, the executive, the CEO, the stay-at-home mum, the mumpreneur: we want to be able to wear lots of different labels and be part of many groups because there are many aspects to who we are and who we could be. If we start making authentic decisions we are likely to feel separate from a group that has originally shaped us and perhaps taken us in as their own or made us feel normal. We feel there may be a part of ourselves that will always be an outsider.

By identifying as the black sheep or the outsider we slow ourselves down, putting the brakes on our inner work. We have an excuse for things not working out. It is a label we can hide behind, keeping ourselves as a self-made victim. We exile ourselves when we don't need to, feeling unaccepted and unsafe. When we take on the right and wrong definitions imposed by culture, society and our social groups we can easily make ourselves wrong. We vote ourselves off the island.

The solution to this self-imposed alienation is to summon up the courage to live life as authentically as possible, which involves a series of actions that can take us on the journey to authenticity. It is a path on which we don't exile ourselves because we think we are different. Can we live without our parents' approval? Are we okay with being a contradiction to those who do not understand: a finance director and a spiritual medium? Can we look at our culture or social groups through more accepting eyes? Can we see the values that join us – love, compassion, forgiveness, gratitude – as opposed to the differences that divide?

At this point in my life I was being *called* to move away from isolation and towards connection with others, but ultimately it was the connection to my authentic self that was the destination I was reaching for.

If we can remove the black sheep label we place upon ourselves we can change our story.

SECOND BEST

Talk to yourself, like you would to someone you love.
BRENÉ BROWN

Women love hard, but we don't always love ourselves as hard as we love other people or other things. We give our best to our families, our jobs and our partners and we give the leftovers to ourselves, to our dreams and purpose. We do it without even thinking, a product of our skills for survival under stressful conditions.

In a study conducted by the University of California, Los Angeles, a group of researchers found the hormone oxytocin is released as a part of the stress response. The release of oxytocin caused females to respond to stress with nurturing and seeking the support of others as opposed to aggression or escape. This hormone, the bonding hormone, buffers or softens the flight or fight response. The female response is to 'tend and befriend'.

We are hard wired to protect whatever social group we belong to, be it a corporation, family, friendship circle or company with a bestselling book. The irony is that these responses are designed to ensure the survival of the collective at the great expense of ourselves.

When we are asked about our lives we answer by saying who we serve, who we love. We do not instinctively speak of our dreams. Our roles come first. What is the impact of this on our life? It's not that we deny every dream we have ever had or completely give all our time away to others. We do, however, turn down the dial on all these things. When a woman does put herself first it is a rare moment and comes with great discomfort. We amplify one part of ourselves and suppress another.

We know that we cannot be half-pregnant: we must completely birth our whole selves into the world. If we don't, well . . . a rage starts to build.

Sometimes you have to walk to the end of a road to realise that it's not that you don't like the destination, but that you wish you had walked it a little differently, that you had stopped and enjoyed the view. I walked down the corporate road as the alpha female; the wild warrior woman was filed away neatly with the annual company board papers and tax returns.

In my time of fifty shades of anxiety I asked: 'How did I end up here?' I had thought that putting my career first was putting myself first. When I stopped and I looked at my life I realised I was unconsciously making choices based on family, society and cultural expectations. How did I end up always feeling like my own desires were secondary in life? Why was there so much guilt at any thought of putting myself first?

Women around me experienced this same conflict and guilt in their lives. Their maternal instinct was usually so strong they couldn't say no. Do we still have an umbilical cord attached to our mothers? To our children? To our jobs? Do these cords need to be cut? Is healthy emotional and physical distance needed? Even if we want to give of ourselves, if we don't find some equilibrium then eventually the taking becomes too much. We become depleted and the result is resentment and, in the end, anger. I realised it didn't matter if I leaned in, leaned out or did the funky chicken dance. I was not consciously making choices, and when I did I was asking permission and seeking approval from others.

I was being called to put myself first.

When we are second best we allow our purpose to be second best.

THE ONE

Some of us are becoming the men we wanted to marry.
GLORIA STEINEM

Women relate to themselves primarily through their romantic relationships: the great holy 'one' in their lives, the lifelong soulmate. That is why for many women their greatest fear is not public speaking or dying, but being alone.

From a young age I bought into the fairy tale myths of relationships and marriage: stability, security and validation from a society that honours having a plus one. I threw myself into finding The One, searching high and low for a man who could support my dreams and not be threatened by them.

As I swiped left and right on dating apps I was unconsciously making sure no man could claim me. I was raising the bar so high that nobody could make the grade. Strong, independent and fierce, I was too scared to belong to a man, too scared to let real and deep love into my life. My image of myself as independent was counterproductive to creating a loving bond with any man. To experience the kind of love I yearned for – which was to be taken care of, nurtured and supported – I needed to give up being in control. This was not a skill I had cultivated.

Most of my relationships up to this point had been toxic, filled with excessive power struggles and disappointment. Soulmates quickly turned to soul hates and wound mates. I stuck around too long to make things work. Unlike my blossoming career, I did not realise men were not projects that could be fixed with hard work.

I didn't want to subscribe to the social construct that valued being a mother over having a career. In pursuing my career I rejected, sacrificed and devalued the feminine within me: my intuition and my vulnerability. I would come home late after working long corporate hours only to find loneliness in my cold bed on a winter's night. I didn't realise I could have both in my life, that they were *not* mutually exclusive possibilities. I didn't want to do life alone, yet I had rejected myself to the point that loneliness was inevitable no matter who I was with or whether I was single or not.

There is a difference between wanting The One and being The One for someone else. There is a difference between wanting The One and being ready to accept them and value them in your life. There is also a difference in picturing The One turning up in life in an exact way, much like a perfectly balanced accounting ledger. Accounting rules did not apply in love, as much as I tried to make them do so.

The One I was looking for was *me*. I wasn't ready to commit to me, so why would any man? After attracting one unavailable man after the next I was called to look within myself and courageously ask: 'In what ways am I unavailable?'

When we are not The One, the one who shows up is no one.

EVOLVE OR DIE

We must be willing to get rid of the life we've planned, so as to have the life that is waiting for us.

JOSEPH CAMPBELL

Change can feel overwhelming. We will do everything in our power to deny change and to stay in the comfort of our ever-growing discomfort. We do not feel we are equipped to manage our evolution and prefer to distract ourselves. We avoid facing the situations and feelings that challenge us, even when confronting them may lead to the growth and expansion we yearn for.

We can spend a lifetime looking for what was already there – our authentic self – but the truth is hidden behind our fears. Those fears contract and cripple us because we believe we need to be too many things to too many people. Our own dreams are folded away neatly with the rest of the laundry.

Ultimately what I was fearing was what would be demanded of me if I followed the Courageous Path. My path to becoming a spiritual teacher and medium would involve studying different spiritual modalities such as tarot, reiki, mediumship and meditation and walking away from my corporate career. I had to bravely create a vibrant life as a single woman. I had to transform loneliness into meaningful solitude. I had to allow myself to make mistakes and learn, to be imperfect and to not be complicit with external expectations. To look different, to do me: my life on my terms. I wasn't ready to be accountable for my choices or even admit that I had choices, so 'stuck' and 'safe' were my preferred uncomfortable options. Like many women I was the victim of my circumstances and I wore a halo as a disguise.

There is a price for evolving: there must be a death of the older version of ourselves and we need to be brave enough to let her go. Our oestrogen and progesterone levels rise and fall like the lunar tides. We move through the stages of life: pre-pubescence, pubescence, peri-menopause and finally menopause. As we grow we have to mourn the loss of one stage and welcome the next. Letting go of our youth is hard, especially when society values the beauty of vitality. Sometimes we betray our hormones, or they betray us, and we find we are unable to have children, we have cancer, we lose our jobs, we lose our marriages or our minds. These circumstances force us to evolve or die – not a physical death, but the death of our dreams.

The thing is, life does not allow us to stand still for very long. When we refuse to move forward it quickly becomes apparent we are starting to go backwards. Our emotions tell us this: we experience depression, resentment, apathy and irritation.

When we ignore signs in our waking life our dreams also start to speak to us, and we start to have nightmares. For me the nightmares were always the same: the sense of running from one empty room to another. The empty rooms represented my untapped dreams and wasted creativity. Every time I was given the opportunity to open another door and walk into another room, the room was empty. The failure in my job made me stop and question why I was having these dreams, and then I woke up not only from the nightmare itself but into my life. I started to remember what I used to dream about when I was younger, what excited me. If we take the small steps to realise our dreams and creative potential in our waking states then our nightmares stop.

I was being called to allow the natural state of my evolution to unfold.

Evolving involves waking up. Are you ready to wake up?

DANGEROUS QUESTIONS

To ask the right question, is harder than to answer it.

GEORG CANTOR

The start of the Courageous Path is paved with Dangerous Questions, which feel dangerous because they call you to your truth. They provide a sense of impending peril – yes, to change the lives that no longer serve you. Early on you negotiate with these questions and try to figure out how to get the life you want without having to give anything up or make any significant changes. You reach for safety by stifling the inner voice that is asking these questions and speaking these dangerous truths. At this stage on the path an alarm is screaming 'danger', so you run back to your old life: work, wine, coffee, prescribed suppressants or anything to silence those Dangerous Questions that might lead you to your inconvenient truths.

The questions only feel dangerous because you are not yet emotionally or spiritually equipped to understand that stepping into the answers will eventually bring you the greatest fulfilment and peace.

At some point you need to be ready to answer the Dangerous Questions. You can only run for so long.

The Dangerous Questions I was too scared to ask were: why did I shut down my intuition all those years ago when I held those tarot cards in the bookstore? Why did I feel so conflicted about whether I should have a corporate career or follow another path? Why was leaving my corporate job to follow my passion so damn hard? Why was finding love so impossible? Why did I feel so conflicted and not ready to step into my journey as a mother?

It would be another seven years before I was able to leap off the corporate ladder with no net to catch me. My Courageous Path would be walked in a thousand steps: some baby steps and some giant leaps. Each step would take me closer to my authenticity.

At the beginning of the path you don't need to act on your Dangerous Questions; you just need to be courageous enough to ask them. You must also be prepared to accept that not all the answers are available to you at this point on the path. Walking the path itself will present the answers you seek. When you are ready to start asking yourself the Dangerous Questions you are ready to start walking forward on your Courageous Path. Be brave and start answering these questions honestly.

Our life is shaped by the questions we ask ourselves.

DANGEROUS QUESTIONS YOU MAY ASK YOURSELF INCLUDE:

1. What am I afraid to change but would have to change to move my life in a new direction?
2. What are my niggling feelings trying to tell me?
3. Which current relationships are best suited to supporting me for the changes I want to make?
4. Whose opinions stop me from moving forward and making changes in my life?
5. What have I learned to be good at that I don't like doing?
6. What is holding me back?
7. How would I feel if my life looked the same in two years?
8. What am I ready to let go of to make a small change now?
9. If I had the complete approval of my friends and family, what would I do with my life?

COURAGEOUS TRUTHS

1. There are many ways to be asleep to your purpose; working long exhausting hours in your job is just one way.
2. Perfection may never be attainable and can be devastating to your self-esteem.
3. Perfectionists can learn how to fail and how to be ordinary yet still loved.
4. When you are second best your purpose is second best. Tired women do not wake up to their purpose.

5. You are called to no longer betray your intuition.
6. If you have made yourself the black sheep you can change the story.
7. You must be The One to find The One.
8. Your awakening cannot be undone.
9. You must be ready to ask the Dangerous Questions that will prompt your truthful answers. These questions feel dangerous because you are at the beginning of the Courageous Path. As you continue to walk on the path you will allow yourself to be curious, and these become get curious questions.

POWER PHRASE

'I have the courage to wake up to my life, my purpose, my calling.'

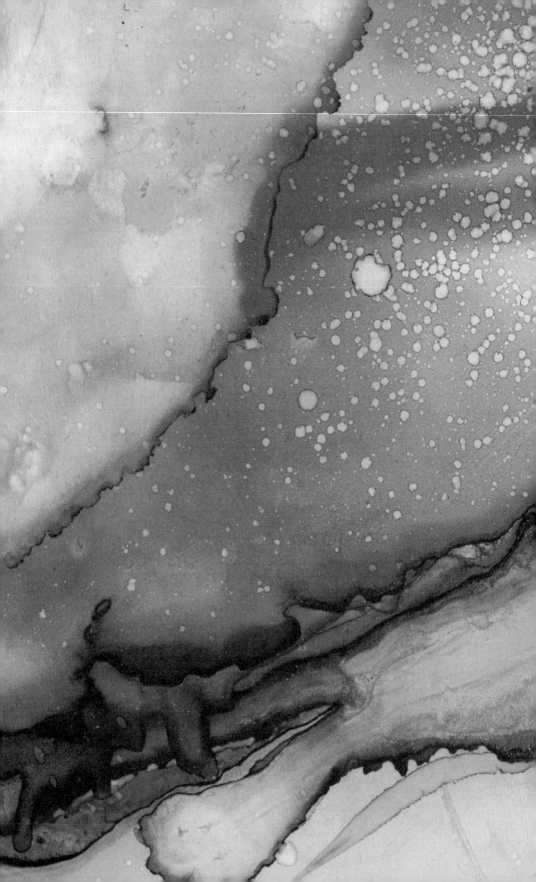

CHAPTER 2

Longing for purpose

If you don't know your purpose then your
immediate goal is to figure that out.

– OPRAH WINFREY

There was a gap between the life I was living and the life I wanted to live, and I didn't know how big the gap was or how to bridge it. This gap was not just about my purpose or my calling: it was my *being* in life. My being was inauthentic.

At this stage on the Courageous Path our job is to identify the gap of inauthenticity. The answers always lie within, yet sometimes friends who have stepped into their authenticity can guide us to where we need to go. We need to listen to their stories.

NATALIE: LEARNING HOW TO CONNECT THE DOTS

The dots always join in the end and nothing is ever wasted.

REBECCA CAMPBELL

In 2015 the adult colouring book trend swept the globe and every publisher jumped on it. Over 12 million adults were tapping into their inner child by embracing mindful colouring. Have you noticed how book publishers like to follow trends? Book titles containing F#CK, celery juicing, F#CK celery juicing and so on. It was a sign of the times that mindfulness was becoming mainstream.

Kaspar Faber, a carpenter born in the 18th century who followed his passion and became the founder of Faber Castell, the world's oldest and largest manufacturer of pens, pencils and art supplies, would have been proud, and not just because most of these adults were colouring in with Faber Castell colouring pencils. Natalie Faber-Castell, Kasper's ninth-generation great granddaughter, was also following her dreams, teaching meditation, mindfulness and sound healing to corporate Australia. She was teaching people how to slow down and refocus their energy by colouring in mandalas – with a Faber Castell pencil if they so chose.

Natalie and I have parallel lives: a high-flying corporate career together with an intuitive side that made us feel different from many. We met during a weekend meditation workshop, and when we first smiled at each other we knew that we shared a similar journey. Our intuition was already speaking to us before we spoke to one another.

After a meditation session I asked Natalie: 'When did you know what you were looking to do with your life?' I wondered if leaving the corporate world and teaching meditation was the simple and final answer, the last stop on her soul purpose train.

For Natalie, the path to her purpose involved no big dramatic moves or single giant leaps. She moved through her life constantly and consistently doing what she loved. She taught music and composition, and worked in and out of the family business in marketing while studying different modalities of meditation. One day all of these skills collided when she came across the modality of sound healing.

'When I found sound healing it made my journey up until now make sense. I thought it had been a collection of incredibly random experiences, but of course it wasn't. I needed all the skills gained from the different jobs and interests when I took up this new passion.'

That is the challenge in finding our soul purpose. Our trained point of reference is to continually look for the linear and simple answer as to what our purpose is, but often the answer lies somewhere on the winding road of small and seemingly insignificant choices we have made along the way. Because here's the thing: we may not have known where those choices, hobbies and fascinations were leading, but our soul did. Our soul always knows. Perhaps we do not have a single purpose but a life filled with multiple purposes all connected, in which fulfilling one purpose leads to the next. Martha Beck describes finding your calling as being 'like tracking a wild animal': elusive, compulsive and constant. Sometimes the journey of our life is the purpose and we must follow the tracks.

We are not looking for our purpose, we are looking for a set of instructions to live our purpose. But what if there are no instructions other than to move forward courageously?

Perhaps sound healing won't be the final destination for Natalie; perhaps it is another significant decision aligning her with another future opportunity, but she will only know this in hindsight. All that matters is that she is in alignment with her heart right now and is always open to possibilities.

The dots need to be on the page of your life before you can connect them. Can you connect the dots in your life?

LISA: TWO HALVES OF HER LIFE MADE HER WHOLE

You're not lost in life. You're just early in the process.
GARY VAYNERCHUK

We don't always know what our purpose looks like. Two halves of our lives can come together to make a whole or, sometimes, our lives are lived in thirds or quarters. The survivor becomes the inspirational speaker; the alcoholic becomes the sponsor; the breathless person becomes the one to show people how to breathe and be still. We may save ourselves first, or be saved and then have the strength and capacity to hold the torch for others. This is what purpose looks like.

The first half of Lisa's life was lived as a Canadian synchronised swimming champion. Like a navy Seal, synchronised swimmers can hold their breath for up to three minutes. They do this with poise and feminine precision, all the while treading water upside down. I met Lisa doing one of her yoga classes and was drawn to her teaching style, which had a sense of discipline and intention as she guided us through our poses. Don't you think all yoga instructors are goddesses? Is it a prerequisite to tick the goddess box when applying to learn this ancient practice? I knew there was a back story so I asked her out, as one does when one wants to sit in the radiance of another.

'Breath is a passion of mine. When I studied yoga I realised that breath impacts everything: our mind, body and nervous system. When I reflect back on the training techniques I was taught as an elite athlete, I realised that the breathing training was done with so much effort. We had to withstand so much pain without any mental tools: no mindfulness, no meditation. We didn't stop.

'Because of the ways I was taught to breathe as a swimmer it means I now have a deep conviction about the way I want to teach people.'

Who would have thought that a Canadian synchronised swimming champion would only learn to breathe later in life?

Perhaps you don't choose your purpose: your purpose chooses you. It just makes sense in the second act of your life. Our scars, wounds, personalities and histories are different. There is nothing more unique to a person than their own authentic path, but many of us will do everything to be like others. We must honour the fingerprint of our soul and look back at what we have learned, evolved through and survived. That becomes our wisdom.

In a live theatre production there are usually two acts, in film there are three and television dramas (unbeknownst to many of us) have four to five acts. None of these acts work as stand-alone pieces as they need the accompaniment of the surrounding materials to grow and develop and to even make any sense.

You might be in the middle of the first act of your life and might feel as though you have been left behind. There is no purpose; no great meaning has shown up for you – yet. You might ask: 'Is there something greater than myself?' But there is a knowing deep within that the challenges, tragedies and hardships you have lived through so far *do* mean something, although it has not yet been fully revealed. You simply need to get through act one and wait for the director to call you to act two. She will whisper in your ear to let you know that the curtain has closed on the first act and the second act is beginning.

Did your first act involve raising a family, birthing a company or start-up or leading a corporate team through difficult times? Perhaps it is time to serve in a different way. In act two you might swap profit motives for soul motives; you might mentor, coach, inspire and lead. The learnings in act one now make sense and prepare you for act two.

So what is your act two? Are you a multifaced, talented and adaptable modern mother ready to spread your wings? In your act two can you bravely dare to live the reality of your dreams and soul purpose? It is not the children who fly the nest; it is the mother. Are you a daring, driven entrepreneur ready to leap into a new unknown? You can spread your wings as a courageous woman. Are you a sleek lioness ready to roar? You've learned to live with stress and uncertainty. You've done the training; now it's time to thrive rather than survive. A bravely lived life has multiple journeys and destinations. Are you ready to fly?

For my yoga friend Lisa, as an elite athlete, successful and breathless was her act one. She stepped into her act two, into her purpose, when she discovered conscious inhaling and exhaling through yoga (pranayama breath). Lisa had been training for her calling since she was born. Perhaps we all have.

Are you in the first or second act of your life?

VAN: THE PURPOSE COMES FIRST

When you are born in a world you don't fit in, it's because you were born to help create a new one.

ANONYMOUS

How often do we know what our purpose is but simply feel it is too hard to follow? We feel too inadequate, that we don't yet have all of the skills, knowledge and wisdom we will need. We feel unqualified to fulfil our purpose and decide to turn our backs on it.

Van is someone you like instantly. We met while doing our MBAs and there was a magnetic pull towards her. We were two peas in a minority pod: she would always take any opportunity to intellectually spar with the lecturers, and 'status quo' was definitely not her middle name. At a smidge under five foot and a lightweight thirty-five kilos, I loved that she would get into the boxing ring three weight division categories above herself and start punching. She is a gentle soul with a tough right hook, and it was not surprising that years later she co-founded a start-up neobank in Australia, Xinja, and later was appointed as an Executive

Director of Xinja Bank, making her one of Australia's youngest Directors sitting on the Board of an Australian Bank. She is a financial disruptor, a woman chiselling a new language into the Rosetta Stone of finance.

'What is self-belief?' I asked as we were inhaling a bowl of pho, a meal that took her back to her humble Vietnamese roots.

'Sheila, with purpose you don't need to believe in yourself.' She stopped mid-mouthful and pointed directly at me. 'You don't have to be the one who's believed in, you don't need to even have the capabilities.'

I was confused: it felt uncomfortable, but I knew she was speaking the truth. My discomfort was in loosening my grip on an old pattern of thinking. I thought I had to have my purpose all figured out, much like the perfectly written MBA assignments we had submitted years prior.

'You just have to believe that what you are doing, your purpose, 'is worthy. Sometimes all it takes is to believe in others, the team around you.'

There are moments when your friends or acquaintances can be your oracle. At this moment Van was that to me. When we believe in our purpose a force of support appears; we don't fulfil our purpose on our own. This idea that it's all up to us is a burden we carry that we need to put down. Pursuing our own authentic purpose in life creates a vehicle for others to pursue *their* authentic purpose. The paths collide, join together and support each other. A team will quickly gather around a shared purpose.

Van did not found new bank alone. She was a co-founder with a group of people who shared a vision to create a bank that acted in the interests of its customers, and to make it easy and fun for people to make the most out of their money. This was her shared authentic purpose.

Are your fears getting in the way of a purpose that may serve many?

KATH: THE POWER OF SELF-BELIEF

It doesn't interest me what you do for a living. I want to know what you ache for, and if you dare to dream of meeting your heart's longing.

ORIAH MOUNTAIN DREAMER

Those who have unearthed their purpose are inspirational. It might be the way they talk with passion about a subject or their approach to life that touches you. When we see their unrelenting conviction to loyally follow their path we are in awe. They have kept the faith and done their best to ignore the noise.

Kath Haling and Keith Urban have two things in common. Their first loves in life were a guitar and music, and later in their careers they both found themselves on a stage in a rural town in Australia as a part of the Tamworth Country Music Festival competition. Kath and Keith followed their own Courageous Paths.

Kath was a storyteller from an early age. At age 11 she performed her first composition at her primary school; unbeknown to Kath at the time, that wasn't something all 11-year-olds were doing. As an adult Kath sang fiercely and wrote song lyrics with even more punch. We first met in a sweaty London pub, singing our hearts out to iconic Australian band Cold Chisel. A song sung together in a foreign land cures homesickness and can bind you for life.

Ten years later, reunited in the corner of a pub in London, Kath and I were at the end of a marathon conversation. It was the last juicy 30 minutes, where tiredness meets honesty. Kath has always had a singular focus, a creative desire that needed feeding. 'There is a fire in my belly. I have tried to deviate, but it just comes back to song writing. I have tried to be an artist in my own right. But my most joyous times are writing songs for other people. I went to film school and ended up writing the film scores for everyone's films. Over time it has become so clear to me.'

Thirty years after her primary school debut, the first musical for which Kath wrote the music and lyrics opened in London on the West End Fringe. I found it interesting that for a woman whose purpose was so clear early on she still had to get a little lost to truly define her calling. The answers were already there in her childhood when she would write song after song, yet she needed to test and prove the idea to herself as an adult. An action of being in purpose may be to test and prove a theory that was revealed to us when we were young.

Our childhood contains so much significant information about what authentically makes us happy. We must be willing to admit that in our childhood we already know the answers to our dreams and how to fulfil our purpose.

Can the answers to your purpose be found in your childhood?

ELLYN: REPAIRING THE WORLD

Fight for the things that you care about, but do it in a way that will lead others to join you.

RUTH BADER GINSBURG

We can often have an impact on the world that goes beyond ourselves.

We wear many hats in a friendship. Ellyn is a psychiatrist: sometimes I am the patient and sometimes the friend . . . and, at other times, the teacher. Ours is a long-distant relationship; we have talked over a Shabbat dinner in Connecticut and a breakfast espresso in Sydney. Despite the time difference we are always in sync. On this occasion we were talking about people having a specific purpose in life and why it is important, and I asked Ellyn: 'What is purpose?'

She said, 'Tikkun olam.'

'What?' I answered, not sure where she was going with this.

'It is a concept in Judaism that means to perform an act of kindness to repair the world. Every soul has a specific purpose, a designated task, that is contributing to the healing of the world.'

Everyone's soul purpose is unique to them. When we acknowledge our soul purpose this is the greatest act of kindness we can give ourselves. When we are in alignment with ourselves we contribute outside of ourselves more readily. There is an expansion of love and joy for those who come into contact with us. This is the repair, the healing we offer to friends, family, community and the world.

When we are following our purpose we are also healing ourselves. When we heal ourselves we can heal the world.

We may downplay our purpose to heal the world and our individual contribution to this cause. We refer to ourselves as 'just a mother' raising a new conscious generation, 'just an energy healer' to the wounded, 'just a yoga instructor' to those needing to come back to breath, 'just a nurse' to those needing to heal their sick bodies. Do you downplay the greater contributions you are making? Can you be brave enough to see your purpose as having a contribution with a large social impact?

How can you contribute to the healing of the world?

HIDE YOURSELF NO MORE

Care about other people's approval and you will always be their prisoner.
LAO TZU

We can quit our jobs, our degrees and our marriages, but we cannot quit our calling. You may step into your purpose, but with a calling you get pulled along.

Many years after surviving the storm that was *Fifty Shades* I found myself contemplating another difficult decision. On the same day I was offered the job as finance director at another major publishing house, Simon & Schuster Australia, I was also offered a regular segment to do live psychic and mediumship readings on a mainstream television network show called *Psychic TV*. By the end of this auspicious day I was a nervous wreck and had not accepted either offer. My parallel paths had converged, and I felt like I had to choose. I also felt like I had to hide.

Choices can cripple us. We get stuck when it appears there are two paths running alongside each other. Here is how things felt for me when I was standing at that particular crossroad.

'Choosing' did not feel like the right step for me to take. Truthfully, being a medium made no sense to me, but my *life* didn't make sense if I didn't pursue that path. Then I realised I did not have to reconcile the paradigm of leaving the corporate world to pursue a spiritual career. I was asking myself the wrong question in needing to choose. This wasn't a fork in the road moment, it was a moment when I could learn to bring two different paths together. I understood there was still so much to learn and experience on both paths – corporate and spiritual. I was starting to gain the insight that my purpose was to bring the different paths together. Years later I would realise that the paths would collide and serve each other as I went on to mentor women in executive and senior management roles to use spiritual tools and their intuition in their corporate jobs and life. But first I had to bravely walk my own Courageous Path.

What causes this conflict over our choices? On one side we have the created identity given to us by the validators: those who have grown us, moulded us, informed us and set us up to be a certain way, to have the identity we've spent a lifetime finessing. The safe side. On the other side we have a scary, shiny, sparkly thing called our purpose. Most of us will veer to the safe side because we've been conditioned from very early on in our lives to do so. For many people there is a point when they want to be brave and courageous enough to swerve onto another path.

The real inner conflict is that we let the created identity shine the brightest, in the process turning down the luminosity of our purpose. When our inner strength emerges to choose another way, that inner conflict lessens just a little.

Here's the uncomfortable truth: all those validators, the ones you think are holding you in a previous mould, are *not* doing that to you. You are doing that to yourself. When I suffered my dilemma, deep down I knew it was time for me to properly come out of the spiritual closet.

Is there a closet from which you need to emerge? Closets are dark and lonely places where the monsters used to live. Our dreams, our transitions and our hopes can hide in the darkness of a closet and, like the darkness of the womb or of the earth in which a seed sprouts, such places bring forth life and also hide the mystery of our purpose.

I realised the beauty of inner conflict is that when it is harnessed and understood it is the fuel that propels you forward. The deep desire to reconcile the conflict is the force that keeps you going and pushes you to make changes in your life.

Attempting to reconcile your inner conflict creates the forward momentum to discovering your authentic path.

The journey to 'whole' is to accept that we are many things in life.

I revealed my spiritual aspirations in my work life because I needed to take action rather than continue to internally complain about the paradox that was my life. I realised that I could move within the opportunities offered to me and elegantly manage the transition. I was trying to get to a destination where my life made sense but came to understand that destinations were pause buttons and would only last for a fleeting moment. My life could make sense at any moment if I allowed it to.

By the end of the week I had agreed to both offers. I didn't know how I would make it work – a finance director by day and on *Psychic TV* at night – but I would. You can't quit your calling.

Inner conflict is a powerful signpost that guides you towards the small steps you need to take to be a fully expressed version of yourself. Ultimately this part of the journey involves shining a bright, bold light on all the facets that make you who you are. It won't be easy, and it will feel uncomfortable. You are moving into a space where no part of yourself is hidden. There will be no eclipses in your life, where part of you is in darkness: you are a radiant star shining bright.

When we stop hiding we stop hiding from ourselves.

COURAGEOUS TRUTHS

1. Living your purpose involves constantly transitioning into work you are curious and passionate about. You may discover that you do not have a single purpose but multiple purposes at the same time, or that fulfilling one leads to the next.

2. You don't always choose your purpose; your purpose may choose you. It may involve overcoming challenges and subsequently doing the inner healing work. You will be called to then share your wisdom. Those who need your wisdom will find you.

3. Your purpose will most likely be bigger than serving yourself and may be to serve a greater cause. Your work is to believe your purpose is worthy.

4. You may have been born knowing what your purpose is; the answers might be found in what you loved doing as a child.

5. Your purpose may be different from your job. You may need to spend time doing both, as both are serving you in different ways. You do not have to choose.

6. Your purpose may be to heal yourself so that you can heal your family, your community or the planet.

GET CURIOUS QUESTIONS

1. What are you passionate and curious about? A clue may be in what you love doing with your spare time.
2. What skills and talents come naturally to you?
3. What hardships and lessons have you learned in your life that may be useful to others?
4. What wisdom and knowledge do you have that can serve in the healing of others?
5. What did you love doing as a child?
6. If you could heal the planet or humans, how would you do it?
7. Do you have a secret passion that few people know about? Who can you share this part of yourself with right now?

POWER PHRASE

'I honour my unique purpose.'

listen, see and feel the universe

In every moment, the Universe is whispering to you.

– DENISE LINN

NECESSITY OF SIGNS

I'm not going to lie: the Courageous Path can be lonely sometimes. Leaving your comfort zone is never easy; it can feel like you're wandering through a darkened tunnel without a torch, trusting that at some point you'll come out the other end. But the truth is, even though it feels like you're alone, you're *not*, and if you're watching for them there will be signs that prove this to you. They will bring you a sense of safety when you need it most.

You don't even need to believe in signs to receive them – the universe is benevolent like that. Here's the cosmic deal: your part of the bargain is to courageously move beyond the relationships that constrict you, the job that offered material security at the expense of your dreams or the home you thought you couldn't replace. In return the universe, the cosmos, God – or whatever you want to call it – will guide you. The walls of that darkened tunnel will have 'Yes, this way' or 'No, go back' etched into them if you just feel, look and listen for the signs.

You can trust in that.

Signs are so vital during this stage of being courageous;
you will always receive them.

BELIEVING IS ESSENTIAL

The leaf of every tree brings a message from the unseen world. Look, every falling leaf is a blessing.

RUMI

There is a catch to the receiving of signs: you have to believe the signs when they come. How often do we receive signs yet refuse to believe them? Exactly.

The question is, why don't we listen. Why do we quickly look away? Sometimes it's because the sign comes to us too easily; it's too obvious or our rational mind can write it off as a coincidence. Sometimes it's because the sign is not what we wanted it to be or how we thought it should show up. And sometimes the sign is subtle: rather than seeing a bus with words in bold print pass us we are instead touched gently by a butterfly in the middle of a busy city. Sometimes there is a sense of disbelief and the awe overwhelms us. Either way, we don't always listen straight away, and even when we do we still may not believe.

The universe will send you signs. Your part of the bargain is to be open to receiving them, to acknowledge them and finally to believe.

AMY: ONLY *YOU* NEED TO BELIEVE IN THE SIGNS

We are not human beings trying to be spiritual. We are spiritual beings trying to be human.

PIERRE TEILHARD DE CHARDIN

I was a year into my job as finance director at Simon & Schuster and working part time as a medium. I used the advantages of my business trips to study and further my spiritual knowledge while travelling the world.

At the end of a long budget meeting in New York, the CEO of Simon & Schuster asked where my travels were taking me next. I was hidden no longer and at a point in my life where I did not need validation from others. Enjoying the credibility my corporate suit offered, I replied: 'To the Omega Institute in upstate New York to study advanced mediumship with James Van Praagh.' The CEO smiled with curiosity.

Hours later I was sitting in the cafeteria at the Omega Institute for Holistic Studies, which is dedicated (obviously) to holistic studies and offers a smorgasbord of experiential, experimental and existential personal development modalities and workshops. I scanned the busy dinner hall searching for a single seat, although I was really searching for a friendly face.

Amy smiled a warm smile and I smiled back. Instant friends, we started talking and discovered that we both worked in publishing. Amy had been the manager and editor of a column called *My Guardian Angel with Doreen Virtue*.

Amy said, 'I read well over ten thousand letters of real-life angel experiences when I was working at *Woman's World Magazine*. At one point we couldn't keep up with the letters coming in.'

My jaw dropped.

Then Amy confessed that when she started out as editor she didn't believe in angels. 'So when did you start believing?' I asked.

'On this particular day I needed to check a Doreen Virtue quote for the column I was editing for her. Usually her publishing house, Hay House, would send copies of Doreen's books to me, but this particular one had not come in, so I headed to Barnes and Noble to buy a copy. I asked a saleswoman to direct me to the Doreen Virtue books. She laughed. "What is going on?" she asked. "Women have been asking for her books for two weeks! We can't keep enough in stock." A chill ran up my spine. The *My Guardian Angel* column had just started publishing two weeks earlier! This was no coincidence; we had caused this run on Doreen's books. I could see it in the mail that was pouring into our office: hundreds of letters, each containing a story. People were inspired and excited by what they were reading in our pages, and now it seemed they wanted to read Doreen's books!

'Here is where the story gets interesting,' Amy continued. 'I headed back to the office and found a big white feather on my keyboard. Honestly, I believed it to be a prank and called out "Very funny" to my work colleagues.'

Amy was sceptical.

I was amused, as Amy, who was literally swimming in angel stories, felt uncertain about the sign that was sitting on her desk. She told me: 'My editor also found a big feather that day under her desk. And for the next ten years I worked on the column, almost everyone who joined our team would receive one – and not always in the office. When my last photo editor started, I told her: "Watch for your feather."' She laughed, but that very afternoon her son stepped off the kindergarten school bus and handed her a big white feather. "This is for you, Mummy," he said. Stunned, she asked him: "Where did you get that?" "The lady said to give it to you," he responded. "Which lady?" Amy asked her son. "I don't know, she just handed me this feather."'

I listened in disbelief as Amy told me her story, and felt my mind engage in a tug of war between believing and not believing.

'Do people believe when they receive a sign?' I asked, wondering if this is the most common question Amy is asked.

'Not really,' she answered. 'Nearly every letter would begin with "This is my angel story . . . maybe this time someone will believe me."'

I was surprised. 'Would having their story published in a magazine make the sign more real for them?'

'Great question. We have been so disempowered from our own authenticity, perhaps we need a witness to our miracles. As if having another person confirm the sign makes it real – a confirmation that they have experienced something extraordinary.'

Amy believes her purpose during that period of working at *Woman's World* was to move from being an editor to being a witness, until finally she was so rooted in the reality of the signs in her own life that she did not need any external confirmation. She did not need anyone to believe her. She did not need my validation. Her faith was unshakeable.

Amy said, 'Miracles and signs changed my life.' They changed Amy's life because they proved to her that she was supported by the universe, which had her best interests at heart. From that belief in the universe's support she went on to become a witness for the reality of this presence in all of our lives, writing books and leading workshops where she teaches people to not only witness the miraculous signs they receive but to honour their scepticism. She tells people: 'Scepticism is guidance – it tells you where you need more proof, more information. So ask for more signs until you can trust that this presence is real, and that it always supports your happiness and well-being.'

We become a different breed when we step onto our Courageous Path; the signs take us further away from our comfort zone. When we share the details, the insights or meaning of the signs, we are speaking the truth to ourselves and being forced to listen to the truth, which can be difficult if we don't want to acknowledge the truth. It is also hard when we are not witnessed or validated. We need to move from needing validation to just believing, because by believing we set up our life for more extraordinary events to occur.

I was at a point on my Courageous Path where I was boldly taking steps to honour both my spiritual and corporate careers. Amy was my sign of validation on that day: she was my white feather.

No one but you needs to believe in the sign. The sign is a gift to you and you alone.

SIGN SHOCK

Souls do not require human language to communicate. They speak with each other through signs, symbols, deep feelings, and poetry!
AVIJEET DAS

There are many books, articles and podcasts about signs and synchronicity. What can never be wholly captured by the written or spoken word is the awe you experience when you receive the sign. The astonishment, disbelief and shock may stop you for seconds, minutes or maybe longer. It isn't the sign that is the most important thing; it is the space after you receive the sign where the real magic happens. After the event, after the awe, a pattern is altered in your life. The drumbeat that you march to changes rhythm or the sound track changes genre. If you are predisposed to 'control freak-itis' you will have a difficult time with surrendering to this information from the universe or even believing that a flow exists that you are not in control of.

The state after you receive the sign is called *sign shock*. It is the space where you inhale and momentarily stop breathing, where the logical mind tries to assert its rationality. It is the moment before you dare to dream. The space is precious and delicate. If you allow yourself to be taken out of the awe of the experience by thinking 'It's not that big a deal' or 'We were meant to bump into each other', the awe will evaporate along with the meaning, information and urgency and the instructions that follow. The sign is meant to evoke emotion, and if you are the logical, too-busy-to-feel type you don't get to absorb the message you are being sent.

If we do not honour the space after the sign we cannot move into asking the important questions. What was the sign showing me? What do I do with this information? What is my truth? These are some of the questions we need to ask after receiving a sign. If we obsess and question the sign and its synchronicity, it can distract us from walking through the doorway towards personal development and spiritual expansion, or from moving into action to make the necessary changes in our life.

Synchronicity of signs relates to coincidences that are meaningful; however, who creates the meaning? *We* must be courageous enough to create the meaning. As the recipient of the sign we are the only one who can do that. We must join the dots to form an arrow pointing to our authentic life. We must be courageous enough to keep going long after the vividness of the sign has faded in our mind.

Harness the space after you receive the sign to ask the questions:
What am I being shown? Why am I being shown?

KATH: SIGNS ARE A REWARD FOR COURAGE

So ... just thought I'd send you a reminder that at this very moment, there are a million eyes upon you, grateful for your courage; that you already know all you need to know; and that whether or not you can see it, you're already soaring. Bravo, The Universe.

MIKE DOOLEY

Finding the courage to chase down our dreams is scary at the best of times. It takes everything we have: every ounce of bravado and strength. We do not need other people adding thinly veiled doubt to the mix as they validate their own choices, yet this is precisely what will happen.

Did you know that you can hear more than 100,000 hours of live music performed by buskers in London Underground stations every year? Did you also know that you need to audition to claim one of the 300 spots available to perform? Busking in the London Underground is a job, a real job.

My friend musician Kath, who we met earlier, was successful in getting one of these spots.

'It's hard when people say to me: "It is so great that you are still chasing your dream." Sometimes it does feel like they are inspired by what I am doing; many times what they are really asking me is: "*Why* are you still chasing your dreams?"' No matter how strong we are, these sorts of words can make us wobbly and doubt ourselves. But here's the thing: while we can't control what other people do and say, we can control how we process it.

As Kath says: 'I have had to accept that when people see you with an open guitar case they see you like you are begging for money. It's their own perceptions they are projecting on to me.

'But there are great days too. Some days I will be performing and I will be questioning "Where is my next move, next creative project?" or I will be waiting to hear back about an upcoming gig from someone. Just yesterday a lady walked past and said: "You are the best busker I have *ever* seen!" I was like: thank you! But I also was thinking "ever seen . . . wow!" And that for me was the universe telling me to just keep going.

'Every now and then someone will *actually* say those words to me: "just keep going", and one hundred per cent of the time I believe it is the universe. Because why would someone say "keep going"? It is a strange thing for a stranger to say. Usually they say "great voice", "great song" or "have a great day." But to say "keep going"? I think that is my mate the universe talking to me.'

You will often receive a sign when you need it the most.

WHY DO WE NEED SIGNS?

A woman's spiritual life is an evolution. She must build it herself.

SARA AVANT STOVER

Many of us require obvious and practical signs before we make any decision to make a change in our life. That's sort of fair enough, because we know that the change is going to require a lot of physical, mental, emotional and spiritual stamina and on some level we want to know that it's definitely worth it, that there's an invisible team there supporting us for when the road gets bumpy and the waves of change grow larger. In those moments when it starts to feel like we are drowning we want to know there is someone we can speak to: possibly the same person who gave you the sign in the first place. When it gets tough we say: 'Hello, universe, remember that sign to quit my job six months ago, the sign that I followed? Well . . .'

When you honour your Courageous Path and your purpose there will be an acceleration in the frequency of signs. This is the validation and guidance the universe promises you. The feeling of being authentic and following your path means that your senses are activated, and they must be activated to follow your destiny. Your intuitive sense of *clairaudience*, or clear hearing, must be activated to hear the sign in another person's voice. For Kath, the signs not only kept on repeating but came to her through many different channels.

Spiritual teacher Colette Baron-Reid describes *cledon* as 'a message from Spirit that is innocently and unknowingly delivered to you by someone or something else. And, once you tune into the *cledons* all around you, you'll be truly amazed at the personal and powerful messages Spirit has for you.' So, when your Uber driver is singing along to a song on the radio and that song speaks directly to you, get curious and be open to hear the messages. When you start to listen, pause and acknowledge the messages they will come to you in the most unexpected ways.

When we believe the way Kath did the sign is activated and amplified. The energy to keep on moving into the next creative project happens and with a greater energy than if the sign had not appeared. Chasing her dream was a courageous choice, but allowing herself to believe the signs directing her was even more courageous. Because of this she felt special, energised, more hopeful and clearer about her path forward.

Some say to the universe: 'I am here, please listen to me.' We do this through meditation, intention setting, gratitude, prayer or just a deep asking wish. And the universe replies: 'I am here, please listen to me.' Both us and the universe are requesting a response. Communication is always a two-way street: we must ask and listen attentively.

We must know that the universe listens to us. We must listen back as it replies.

Knowing this, we can empower ourselves to believe we can be a sign bearer for others on their own Courageous Path. You will give signs and words of affirmation and point the lost in the right direction. We can all be light bearers.

When Kath sings Adele's 'Make You Feel My Love' in the London Underground, perhaps she is giving a sign – a message they need to hear – to one of the many London commuters on their trip home.

A sign is a reward for courage.

POINTING TO YOUR DESTINY

There's no such thing as a meaningless coincidence.

DEEPAK CHOPRA

Some synchronistic events are instructive and carry great meaning. They are not random, although we may be left scratching our heads when they occur. But they are real. The message, the information, the pointer is undeniably, unmistakably, unshakeably and so obviously true. We don't have to do a lot of thinking with such synchronistic events as the thinking gets in the way, adding too much or taking away meaning. When we feel we are in a profound synchronistic event or sequence we just know. It is that simple.

Why are we scared to take on the mystical with absolute certainty? Because it is invisible or can't be proven? Are we waiting for science to prove it exists? Who created the race between science and the invisible forces anyway? These pursuits are running a different race at different speeds.

In my early 30s I was very afraid of death. Not of dying myself, but of other people dying and of the incredible emotions of grief and loss. I was scared of being the one left behind to grieve, overtaken by emotions I was incapable of understanding. I was also scared of the supernatural. Superpowers that women have can feel scary, especially when we don't have awareness or mastery of them.

The universe sent me love and death together as a synchronistic event; it knew I was only going to overcome my fear of death through love. The universe sent me four partners in a row (yes, four!), each of whom I loved in different ways. The only thing these four men had in common was that they had each lost a sister to death: accident, illness, sudden or expected. Soon I learned through these men that life, love and the family unit goes on in so many different ways after death, and that was my initiation into becoming a medium. So many mediums have an unusual and early loss in their personal lives. I was spared this; however, the universe taught me in another way.

Because of love and the need to understand these men and their personal experiences I read books about death, including research done by Elisabeth Kübler Ross, who coined the five stages of grief, and Eastern philosophy, including the profound teachings within *The Tibetan Book of Living and Dying*. I asked myself many questions, and without being aware of it I was in training to be a medium. This synchronicity prepared me so that years later I could sit with the bereaved and hold them and their grief. I was no longer scared of death and dying.

A sequence of synchronistic events makes you stop and think. When I questioned if I was really meant to be a medium and if this was my life path, synchronistic events provided an answer that made me feel certain at my core. Synchronicity changed my view so I started seeing the world differently. Most importantly, the signs didn't show me everything that would have been too overwhelming. I was shown just enough, which is what synchronicity towards your destiny looks like: a small, dense cluster of information to tell you what you need to know, but not more than you can handle.

Synchronicity, purpose, destiny: this trifecta is only understood in hindsight and we must be patient.

Synchronicity will point you to your purpose.

WRONG WAY. GO BACK!

Of course you didn't see the red flags. You were using them as a blindfold.

ERIN VAN VUREN

A sign can stop you when you are off course.

The change threshold, is exceedingly high. Days can be filled with monotony, serious conflict, bullying at work or a loveless marriage, yet we stay put and grounded in a reality that feels familiar and highly unrewarding. I have looked back and been appalled at how high my pain and fear thresholds were. Quite impressive, actually: gold medal stuff. But if the signs come and we still ignore them we are denying the universe a voice that seeks to help us. We are stuffing cotton wool in our ears like a petulant child. But here's a little secret I learned the hard way: the universe will have its way. If you don't listen to it, it will ensure it is heard.

Michael Kors is a fantastic brand. I own multiple handbags, shoes and dresses from this iconic brand. Many years ago when I was leaving a job interview there was no white feather or butterfly landing gently on my arm as a positive sign. Instead, my brand new Michael Kors handbag strap cleanly and swiftly snapped in two, leaving me standing in the centre of Sydney and staring at my inexplicably broken handbag. My gut instinct was yelling, insisting I say no to the job if I was offered later. The pedestrian walk sign had turned green and I didn't move; I was frozen still, staring at the grey strap. The handbag was so new I could smell the distinct scent of new leather, a smell that made the sign even more obvious.

Like the strap, was the job going to break me into two pieces?

It was the third round of interviews, and my ego was doing star jumps. I was telling myself: 'You are amazing, you have survived round three in the ring!' I was up against one other candidate and my highly competitive nature was saying: 'You need to win!'

However, my intuition was telling me that this was not the right next job. My intuition was telling me to get on the soul train and start doing my soul work. I didn't exactly know what that looked like, but I sure knew what it wasn't: a pay rise, more demanding hours and an entirely new stratosphere of stress. Owning up to the assignment of my soul at this point meant downsizing my job, salary and perceived status and investing time in my spiritual pursuits. It meant going against what society had conditioned me to do.

The snap of my handbag strap was a big sign that I chose to ignore.

We dismiss our powerful intuition and don't recognise how in sync we are with the universe, that a sign could be specifically for us and trying to point us in the right direction. For many this is a completely foreign concept. The truth is the signs we receive will vary; they will be big, small, obvious and discreet. Regardless, we must listen. We also don't listen to the most obvious signs because we are not ready. I was not ready because I had not done personal development work to understand the source of my limiting beliefs, the deepest source of my fears.

So, yes, I am speaking from experience. I turned my back on the big neon Super Bowl sign from the universe and accepted the job, but would pay a hefty price for this decision 12 months later. It was a long 12 months of anxiety and depression and a lot of pretence that I was in an amazing job with an amazing company and loving my life. My social media life was fabulous! The reality was the opposite.

On many a workday morning as I turned my computer on I thought about the handbag and wondered why I had ignored that sign.

Don't ignore the stop signs. All signs are benevolently guiding you.

COURAGEOUS TRUTHS

1. Signs are vital on the Courageous Path and you will receive them.
2. Believing the signs is essential.
3. Only *you* need to believe in the signs.
4. When you receive a significant sign you may experience sign shock. Pause and ask: 'Why have I been sent this sign? What does it mean?'
5. Acknowledging the signs with gratitude invites more signs in.
6. Signs are a reward for your courage.
7. Synchronicity will point you to your purpose; there are no accidental coincidences.
8. A sign can show you that you are off or on track.

GET CURIOUS QUESTIONS

1. Do you believe the universe sends you signs? Why?

2. Do you ask the universe for signs? If not, what sign would you like to ask for and what question will the sign be answering?

3. Have you experienced sign shock? If so, describe the time you experienced this.

4. What signs have you been given that you have ignored in the past? What was the outcome?

5. Have you regretted ignoring signs?

6. Can you recall a time you received a sign and acted upon it? How did it feel? What was the outcome?

BE STILL PRACTICE: HOW TO RECEIVE SIGNS

You can request the universe or source energy around you to give you a definitive yes or no answer to a question. Here is one approach to try out for yourself:

*   Close your eyes and centre yourself in your own bubble of white light.

*   Think about the issue or problem you need guidance on, and slow your breath as you think about it to allow for focus and concentration.

*   Request in your own inner voice: 'Universal spirit, please help me to understand best if I should commit to this choice ahead of me?', or 'Please send me a clear and direct sign to proceed with this choice' or 'Please advise me on how I should resolve the issue I am facing.' Sometimes at the time you make the request to the universe your inner connection to your higher self will provide you with the information in the moment, which may be experienced as a sense of clarity and a flow of thoughts. Be open and receptive to receive the sign(s). The universe may come back quickly with a sign of confirmation or it might send you a series of synchronistic signs that confirm themselves over a few days.

*   After you receive a message or a synchronicity event from the universe you need to be humble and give thanks for it. Genuine gratitude from deep within your heart is important, as you are telling the universe you are listening and acknowledging its help. This will reinforce the power of your requests the next time you want guidance and help.

POWER PHRASE

'I am grateful for the abundance of signs I receive from the universe.'

CHAPTER 4

The Courageous Leap

I see your pain and it's big. I also see your courage, and it's bigger. You can do the hard things.

– GLENNON DOYLE

At some point on your Courageous Path your soul will cry out for you to take a Courageous Leap in a new direction. Whether it is big or small, it will feel like an enormous leap into the abyss. You won't yet know that you are moving closer towards your purpose or that this leap is part of a larger plan for your life that is starting to take shape, but you will know that the authentic life you are seeking can only be reached when you leap.

You may be around friends or family and need to provide an explanation such as 'I am leaving my marriage', 'I am starting my side hustle', 'I am off to study ecstatic dance in Bali for a week' or 'I am quitting medicine.' Fear can't be quantified and will be experienced on some level regardless of the size of the leap.

The leap may not always be about your career or purpose work, but it will ultimately lead you to your greater purpose.

Leaping will feel uncomfortable, which it has to as we are being called to make a change in our predictable and unfulfilled life. We have an inkling or a knowledge that we have a purpose and are ready to step away from our resistance. The leap may involve starting something new, such as an interest, passion or something our friends tell us we are talented at. It may be the thing we loved or did before we had kids or when we were kids.

The leap may also be to stop something: to leave a marriage that was over years ago, to suspend your once-fulfilling corporate career, stopping IVF or ceasing the side business hustle.

The Courageous Path may feel lonely and scary and sometimes failure feels certain, but the leap requires spiritual courage. We have forgotten how to leap and must return to the past and remember a time when faith met our fear and fulfilment followed.

DON'T LOOK (TOO MUCH) BEFORE YOU LEAP

Do you really want to look back on your life and see how wonderful it could have been had you not been afraid to live it?

CAROLINE MYSS

Choices terrify people. Most of us will do a lot to delay making decisions. We need to revisit the Dangerous Questions we asked ourselves at the beginning of our Courageous Path one last time before the leap. These are the questions that, when asked and answered with utter honesty, deliver a true and clear way forward that is undeniable. We now know that self-awareness leads to greater insight, yet insight in action is where the real change happens.

In the past these questions stopped us: can I continue the status quo for the next decade? The same career? Apathy in my marriage? The unspoken words in my relationships with my parents? Hiding my spiritual gifts? Pretending that I am okay with my daily sacrifices? If nothing changed in my life, could I be happy in one year, three years or five years? If I waited, what change in the future would make me more prepared for the Courageous Leap?

We are now ready to answer these questions and then to leap! Some questions can be answered before the leap, while others need the leap to occur before being answered.

As children we are told to look before we leap. As adults, what are we actually looking for? Rarely is it real and present danger; quite often it is the small voice of fear or *perceived danger* that stops us. Sometimes we need to *not* look before we leap, to *not* look for a reason not to leap. Our mind can manifest the leap as a danger, and that imagined danger is fuelled by a fear that stops us.

Stop looking; you have seen enough. You are ready.

ARE YOU A TYPE A OR TYPE B?

The greatest danger for most of us is not that our aim is too high and we'll miss, but that it is too low and we will reach it.

MICHELANGELO

In 1976 two inquisitive cardiologists, Meyer Friedman and Ray H. Rosenman, discovered two different personality types when they needed to re-upholster their waiting room chairs a little too frequently. Mr Upholstery said: 'There's something different about your patients: I've never seen anyone wear out chairs like this.' The cardiologists discovered that, unlike most patients, who wait patiently, the anxious, squirming, cardiac patients were unable to sit in their seats for long and wore out the arms of the chairs much more quickly. Having a sample of clients with such a strong predisposition for heart disease allowed them to formulate a clear distinction of a particular type of personality. Five years later, their formal research provided two distinct personality group types: A types (their cardiology patients) and their opposite, B types.

If you are an A type personality you have rarely failed in life, with the cost of adrenal fatigue. You are out of practice in allowing yourself to fail and may possibly one day find yourself in the waiting room of a cardiologist. You must be prepared to fail but you also need to know that you are not the failure.

If you are a B type personality you have rarely danced on the knife's edge in life or allowed yourself to succeed in a big audacious goal. The risk of shining too brightly is uncomfortable for you. You are out of practice in contemplating success and must be prepared to stand out and succeed.

We all sit on the continuum between types A and B and must be prepared to risk succeeding and to risk the experience of failure.

When you leap don't expect instant success and don't expect instant failure.

The Courageous Path lies somewhere in the middle, in the grey zone, that feels uncomfortable. Remember it is a path and not a destination, so you must find comfort in just being on that path. When you commit yourself to a fitness goal and are waking up in the dark mornings to train, you thought it would be easier. When you start your new business and the months roll on as your savings deplete, you thought it would be easier. When you leave your marriage and your plus one is now a zero and you're lonely, you thought it would be easier.

We must be prepared to sit in the void, the space where we leave behind who we were to create the possibility of becoming who we need to become. We need to know why we are leaping, so that in these moments on the other side we can find inner peace and know that the Courageous Leap is taking us to where we need to go in the future.

Why are you making the leap? Again, why are you making the leap?

The 'why' never goes away; we just get better at answering it and being okay with the answers.

THE LEAP IN ACTION

The important thing is to be able at any moment to sacrifice what we are for what we could become.

CHARLES DU BOS

We all have secrets, don't we: the deepest wishes for our soul? We need to let our supressed joy guide us to be truly authentic and free.

Many years ago I was standing on my career ladder straining my neck as I stared up at the next rung; completing a company director's course was the next right move to make . . . or so I thought. The promise upon completion was 'understanding risk and strategy, financial literacy and board effectiveness'. It was also the promise of stability. But it didn't *feel* like the right move. Even though I wasn't aware of it, I was starting to make decisions from my heart. The next right move had nothing to do with my career and everything to do with my life and what brought me joy.

I made the conscious choice to turn the corporate ladder around to become horizontal. Like a curious monkey I started to swing, and The Arthur Findlay College was where I wanted to study next. The Arthur Findlay College in England is an institution for studying the practice of being a medium. Arthur Findlay, its founder, was a writer, accountant, stockbroker and medium, who came out of the psychic closet to his stockbroker buddies. As he took the leap he created an incredible legacy that made it so much easier for those following his spiritual path. For me, becoming a medium was still a secret. As my eyes scanned down the list of courses taught at the college a buzz of excitement ran through my body.

This is what the leap feels like: electricity running through your body.

There is much to learn, many friends to make and a new version of yourself to discover on the other side of the leap. That is where you are leaping to: a more expanded version of yourself. The leap is just the action, sometimes a propulsion away from an older version of yourself that you have become tired of.

It was a leap of faith for me in that moment to press the 'Book now' button. I had been thinking and dreaming about studying at this college for months but had never considered moving into action to follow the dream. This felt new. Even when new is good for you it still feels uncomfortable, unfamiliar and potentially unsafe.

As I entered my credit card details my fear turned to excitement. The same chemicals are released when we experience fear and excitement, the same heart palpitations and sweaty armpits. It is just the pattern of thought after the initial rush of adrenaline that creates the emotion of fear or excitement. My first thought after I booked was: 'OMG, I cannot wait to go! This is going to be the most incredible week.' The next thought was: 'What will I tell my family and friends?' Excitement and fear are bedfellows. I was still building up my spiritual self-esteem; it would take time.

Regardless, I had taken the leap.

The new choices you make can feel exhilarating, uncertain and scary: it is meant to feel that way. However, despite the confusion, the decision will still feel right.

KATE: FAST LEAPS THAT FEEL RIGHT

Don't be surprised at how quickly the Universe will move with you once you have decided.

JORDAN BACH

I was sitting in a café waiting to meet Kate and time travelling back to my earliest memory of her. We went to school together but weren't close friends. She was blonde, blue-eyed and cherubic, while I was foreign, buck-toothed and just a bit too smart. We had circled each other through school: 'East is East and West is West and never the twain shall meet,' said Rudyard Kipling. This was our childhood and adolescence.

Twenty years later, Facebook brought Kate and me together. A random message and some toing and froing over a number of weeks grew to plans to meet in person. I was still a teenager and quite nervous.

We started with the basics, filling each other in on where we were in our lives. Kate was a police officer, a first responder: she was the first to arrive and provide assistance at the scene of an emergency. She was also a mother of four, married and living in Sydney. Courage was her middle name. She was alert, hypervigilant and tired.

Our conversation quickly hurdled over the trivial and soon we were speaking from our souls. Friendships on the Courageous Path develop fast because we hold the secret key to unlock each other's worries, fears and blocks. The friendship provides a validating mirror.

Kate spoke of the leap she had taken to head in a new direction: she had decided to go on a short trip to Chicago. Her decision didn't quite make sense in my mind, because as with our shared childhood I was still trying to make everything fit into predictable, perfect boxes.

'I have seen a lot of death and loss in my career and on this particular day I could not shut the negativity out. I was at home with my husband and he saw me reaching for the wine as an instant fix. He told me to go to yoga, knowing I always felt better afterwards.

'After an intense Bikram yoga session I was lying down listening to the voice of the teacher and thought: "This has actually made me forget about my horrendous day and brought me calm." It was like nothing else could get me to that place.

'When I was back on nightshift I googled "yoga" and "police"; I don't even know why I did! "Yoga for first responders" came up.'

How many times has Google propelled us with lightning velocity onto our soul path? Out of nowhere we just Google something, divinely inspired, and Google takes us where we need to go. The Courageous Leap for Kate was where grace met guts. She was shown the way and she took the leap.

Kate immediately booked the course and her flights to Chicago, and became the first international policing student to attend Yoga for First Responders. Thirty per cent of first responders experience post-traumatic stress disorder, and this yoga technique is designed to radically calm the nervous system. Kate began changing the lives of first responder police personnel in her community, taking them from depression to downward dog. Her kids and husband had her back because she believed in her decision.

She had the courage to take the leap.

Do not look around for validation to leap. You do not need validation.

MID-LEAP

Making decisions is a key anxiety trigger. If we drill down a bit we can see that this happens because we work to the belief there's a perfect decision out there to be made. But such a thing doesn't exist. And clutching at something that doesn't exist is enough to send anyone into a drowning panic.
– SARAH WILSON

We fear so much what others will think of us that we stop sharing our stories of Courageous Leaps. When we don't share the energy the leap can wane. Mid-leap I wondered whether it was possible to be a medium and still be respected in the corporate world. I was looking for a step-by-step guide although none existed, but I was learning that the dummies guide lay within. As I leaped out of one life and into the next life I was airborne between two versions of myself: ungrounded and unanchored.

'So where are you going for your vacation, Sheila?' a work colleague asked me. I panicked. I shrank. I was paralysed when asked this question because I wasn't yet prepared to be truthful with myself and to the world. How could I say I was going to The Arthur Findlay College to study mediumship?

Our fears are always much worse than reality. When I did share my plans some people were intrigued, gathered close and asked more questions, while others were indifferent and could not have cared less. They were more worried about who would cover the workload when I was away.

The corporate world is a separate world where masks are worn and the secrets of our highest desires are hidden, except for the brave ones who dare to share. We can all benefit when we take our masks off.

Going to The Arthur Findlay College to study mediumship when I was reaching an apex in my corporate career or should have been starting a family made no sense to anyone, even myself, but my strong intuition and overwhelming feelings were telling me it was the right thing to do. 'You want to spend a week's annual vacation to speak to the dead in the cold of England?' The truth is that when I went my heart was filled with so much warmth, and talking to the dead ironically made me feel the most alive I had felt in a long time.

The aliveness you feel is the sign that the Courageous Leap is right.

LANDING AFTER THE LEAP

For the things we have to learn before we can do them, we learn by doing them.
ARISTOTLE

Landing after the leap can feel like landing in a foreign land, and you will feel different. Sometimes the leap is not an *Eat, Pray, Love* tale; it is a starve, panic, cry experience. All leaps do not turn out okay immediately, and while the other side of the leap may be a bit messy it is still the right side.

Like Harry Potter running through platform 9 ¾, I too ran through an invisible wall of fear with great courage and on the other side I found Hogwarts School of Witchcraft and Wizardry (or its equivalent). There was no Gryffindor House but instead clusters of international students with an uncommon bond of studying this mystical craft. Some leaps involve travelling far and running through solid brick walls, and courage is the only tool you need during these moments.

While growth does not always equal immediate success it does lead to expansion, and expansion leads to a fuller expression of who you are.

After you leap your previously blurry vision will become 20/20 vision. People around you will start to ask: 'How did you do it?' You become a torchbearer and have now joined a new team: the *brave ones*.

Once you build up your courage you will have the strength to take many more leaps.

Leaps tend to cluster together as forward momentum is created. You will rarely be called to make just one leap and will need to keep leaping forward. That is unless the negative self-belief takes hold. For some the old patterns will again prevail, and even when we are on purpose many question it. Am I living according to my purpose or my calling? Is there still a bigger version of myself to be accessed? The dreams we wanted to manifest have now finally appeared, though we forgot that they were once dreams and a leap to be created. We often don't believe our dreams can come true. When they appear we forget they were once a wish and a desire. We are on the next stage of our courageous journey and are called to be more yet again.

We soon realise that our purpose is not a destination but a series of leaps, events, pit stops and a continual call to access a more truthful part of ourselves as a continual practice.

YOU ONLY NEED TO MAKE SENSE TO YOURSELF

If not you, who? If not now, when?
PRIMO LEVI

Some of the courageous decisions and actions you take are not going to make sense to your family and friends. The outcomes are unknown, and those around you will be seeking to understand the goal you are reaching for or the prize at the end of the race: the safe knowns.

Sometimes the questions asked hurt: 'Why would you give up your career?', 'Have you not considered the impact on your kids?' or 'What will you do for money?' These questions undermine us at a time when we are vulnerable and need external validation. They can weaken our resolve if we allow them to.

We have already asked ourselves these questions and have done our best to answer them. 'Everyone will be okay'; 'I don't need to keep sacrificing myself'; 'It is time I give back to myself'; 'I have given up on my dreams for too long'; 'I cannot wait any longer'; 'It will never be the right time; now is the right time.' And sometimes the answer is 'I just don't know, but this feels right' and that's totally fine – you are willing to discover the answer.

There can be a language of regret but there is also a sense of urgency to take this leap. You are facing forward and are ready to move on. You may not always have the strength to say certain words out loud, allowing the truth to be spoken, but do not allow time and excuses to get in the way. Brené Brown, author of *Braving the Wilderness*, writes: 'Do not think you can be brave with your life and your work and never disappoint anyone. It doesn't work that way.' The leap for a woman is powered by reclaiming who she is. Just take the leap. There are no guarantees: there is no wrong and it will feel right.

Following your heart feels like a luxury and you may be made to feel like it is an indulgence It is not. When I told my father I was quitting my corporate job I again became the little girl seeking permission. 'You can't be happy all the time in your job,' was his sympathetic and instructive response. I knew this, having lived through the corporate experience for many years, but being happy so little of the time wasn't enough to sustain my life force.

The challenge with the decision to leave my corporate job was that my unsure self constantly yearned for validation and acceptance from my family. Success in the corporate context has a narrow definition. The material definition does allow mortgages to be paid off, nice hotels to be stayed in and the fix of online shopping, but what happens when you have an awakening or a nervous breakdown or you lose your job? You are then summoned by the universe to redefine what success means to *you*. That might actually mean leaping out of the corporate world and honouring yourself when perhaps few others will honour you.

I finally quit my corporate job to serve full time as a medium, spiritual teacher and mentor. This leap was one of those giant leaps and I felt for a long time as though I was airborne.

It was time to follow my heart. Some leaps are little and some big, but this felt enormous. Perhaps all leaps that involve honouring yourself feel like giant leaps, but the secret to taking the leap comes from the platform of inner strength and resilience you build on for many years.

Following your heart is not a luxury; it is a necessity.

UNIVERSAL LEAPS

Almost everything that you want is just outside your comfort zone.

JACK CANFIELD

Tarot readings are back in vogue. Of the 78 cards in the tarot deck The Fool is one of the luckiest, symbolising new beginnings and a leap of faith. Unlike the other cards in the deck it has no number and is either the first or the last card of the major life path cards, depending on your interpretation of the leap. Our Courageous Leap can be the beginning of our journey or it can mark the end of a long and arduous road, but the leap is needed to create a much-needed change of direction. One of my earliest spiritual mentors carefully explained the intricacies of the symbology on the cards to make this important point to me. The man on The Fool card was carrying a knapsack containing everything he needed, which represented universal knowledge. There was a white dog at his feet, representing loyalty, protecting him as he learned his lessons. The mountain in the backdrop symbolised the challenges yet to come. The Fool archetype is focused on the leap.

I wondered how one simple card could illustrate so much that is universal about the leap of faith? I had yet to leap, so the learnings were yet to come. How timeless is the leap? The Italian nobles of the 1400s would have seen this card when playing the parlour game of tarrochi and known it represented success and encouragement on their journey forward. When The Fool is placed in front of you, you are anything but a fool. When you take the Courageous Leap it is the greatest act of self-love.

We are all called to leap.

COURAGEOUS TRUTHS

1. Stepping into your purpose will mean you have to take Courageous Leaps.
2. Your answer to the question 'Why do I need to leap?' will give you conviction when leaping.
3. When you land you will feel exhilarated and have a sense of certainty that you are at the next stage on your Courageous Path.
4. Your Courageous Leap only needs to make sense to you.
5. Keep leaping, as the Courageous Path will call on you to make continual leaps.

GET CURIOUS QUESTIONS

1. When was the last time you had the courage to take a big leap in your life? Why did you leap? Describe the leap you took.
2. What is the reward you received as a result of the leap?
3. What regrets do you already have from not taking a leap in your life?
4. What leap do you wish for and dream of taking? What could your life look like in the future if you were to leap?
5. If you did not leap, are you prepared to keep on living your life exactly as it is now? How do you feel about this?
6. If you leap what is the worst thing that could happen? Who is already there to support you if the worst thing did happen?
7. What is one small leap you can make that will take you closer to your big leap?

POWER PHRASE

'I am ready to take my Courageous Leap.'

CHAPTER 5

Soul tribes

The ache for home lives in all of us, the safe place
where we can go as we are and not be questioned.

— MAYA ANGELOU

ARE YOU A LOCUST OR A GOOSE?

Locusts move in a swarm and geese move in a V-shape formation when they
migrate to find new food sources. To an outsider it looks as though the locusts
and geese are moving as a collective or a tribe and have a common purpose
and vision. Don't families sometimes look like that in life, moving together
harmoniously and supporting each other, with each validating their collective
beliefs and values?

What the external world sees isn't always the truth. Both the geese and locusts
are surviving, but are they *thriving*? Is the individual purpose of each member of
the swarm or flock being supported? Sometimes the collective beliefs of the tribe
you are moving with do not align with your own individual beliefs, and there
is a false impression of belonging to this tribe. You may not truly belong, and if

you *try* to belong it will make finding, following and creating your authentic life incredibly difficult if not impossible.

Research has shown that the mass migration of locusts is strongly influenced by the fear of being bitten from behind: locust swarms are formed because the individual locusts are desperate to stay a step ahead of their cannibalistic fellows. The individuals that fail to continue moving forward are likely to be attacked and risk becoming a source of protein for others in the swarm. Yes: you fear your fellow locust will eat you alive if you do not continue to move forward and follow the rules!

Do you feel like a locust within your current family, social group or work environment? You may be moving forward in life, but are you motivated by a fear of belonging to a swarm that does not serve you? Are you trying to survive or to fit in? Are you trying to avoid being consumed by the collective limiting beliefs that don't work for you any more?

The V-shaped formation that geese fly in enhances communication and coordination, and because of this the birds beat their wings less often and thus conserve energy on a long and difficult journey. Also, to keep things fair, geese take turns being in the front, with each bird moving to the back when they get tired.

Like geese, when you flock with your soul tribe they will support you and fly in a V formation with you when the winds in your life change direction. They will allow you to rest and recuperate when you need to and the journey to where you are going will be much easier. Also, you will provide the same support to them and make their journey easier. By being in a flock with your soul tribe the individual purpose of each member will be served.

Are you a locust or a goose? How are you moving in your tribe?
Do you need a new tribe?

It might be a slow process to admit to ourselves that some friendships, work colleagues, family members or partners may have stopped serving us or maybe never did, and we have moulded ourselves to suit the situation. One of the scary prospects of walking the Courageous Path is that we stand to find out who really supports us and who doesn't; however, when we do, we free ourselves from limiting beliefs and allow ourselves to find a home elsewhere – perhaps within ourselves.

If you know you need to find a new tribe you may feel as though you are carrying out an act of betrayal for flying away, but you aren't. You are being authentic, and this courageous action may be needed to walk away or take temporary exile. By staying put, by persuading people to be on your team, you are waiting for their approval. As you stand waiting you engage in emotional servitude to the old tribe. You must recognise those who fully support your quest for purpose and a life of meaning and those who do not.

With a tribe that is not authentically your own you may encounter people who want you to be a mirror for them. When they look at you they want to see themselves and you will contort, twist and shrink yourself to make this possible, but like a difficult yoga position you can't hold this pose for too long. So what do you do? You take long, deep breaths, then all of a sudden, you will say 'Enough!'.

Sometimes our family of origin is not our soul tribe. That is okay.

When you are honest about who is in your current tribe you begin to acknowledge who you need around you to help create your authentic life and what changes you need to make; thus the search for the soul tribe who supports you begins. When you follow your true path you are never alone, for it is a promise from the universe that it is filled with people who support you every step of the way.

FINDING WHERE YOU BELONG

You won't meet a friend sitting on your couch.
REESE WITHERSPOON

Even a lone wolf wants to belong. And sometimes our quest to belong can be born from alienation. We may have been cast adrift from our own family or taken voluntary exile, the adult version of time out. It is hard to admit, but one of the strongest needs for every human being is for love and community. If this sense of belonging is absent then isolation will be mostly what we know.

It is common to wait for an invitation to join a new tribe, but we cannot wait for an extended hand. We are not separate from others on their Courageous Paths: there is an invitation for the paths to merge. Our longings for connection will only continue to grow and we must seek out the group or individuals seeking us, which is where connections, answers and healings will be found. Perhaps we need to open our hearts to consider what possibilities can be experienced with a group of people who see us differently, which will then allow us to see ourselves differently. To step forward and make change we must ask ourselves what parts of our life we need more support in.

When you do find your new soul connections and tribe you will be freed from the sense of isolation and being misunderstood in your old world. You will be encouraged by your common longing to share yourself authentically. Initially, this is the glue that is needed. The world is full of sisters, brothers, fathers and mothers who want to create a new soul tribe around you and with you. You must become the seeker of them.

Your soul will guide you to your soul tribe. But you must courageously venture out.

WITNESSED AND HELD

A circle of wise women is an archetype in itself.

JEAN SHINODA BOLEN

A women's circle is the manifestation of a soul tribe. It is a safe, sacred space for women to come together to be heard, seen and felt. Inner secrets will be shared. The most important thing about these soul tribes is that shame will be shared. We need to find a tribe to share our deepest, darkest secrets to help us move through them.

MELINDA: YOUR SOUL TRIBE SUPPORTS YOU

Friendship is born at the moment when one person says to another, 'What! You too? I thought I was the only one.'

C.S. LEWIS

After 18 rounds of drugs and years of grieving, a fertility specialist told Melinda Rushe, author of *Regain Control of Your Fertility Journey*, to give up, so Melinda found a way to live a little lighter and breathe into the destiny her fertility journey offered her. Later she began running women's circles to guide women on their challenging fertility journey. I met Melinda during an executive coaching workshop, and was curious about her journey.

'I see every ethnic diversity, every age. You can't say it is *this* type of person this happens to. That is what is so amazing in coming together as a group. You look around at twenty people in the room and you realise we are all coming from different places, yet we all have the same intention of having a baby. It is quite inspiring. So much of this journey is isolating.'

As she spoke I recalled the shame I felt at the time of freezing my eggs, a process referred to as *social freezing*. I felt society branded me as indulgent because I was delaying having a family. I didn't want to be judged as a corporate go-getter, so I only told my close friends and alone I administered the hormone injections every night.

The egg-freezing process is precise and orderly: the final egg retrieval can only happen when a trigger injection is administered exactly 24 hours prior, and you are given a 15 minute window to administer the injection. This critical trigger injection collided with an important board meeting I had to attend, and I recall thinking: 'How can I change the time of the trigger injection with the IVF clinic?' Yes, work came first again over my personal life. I could have been vulnerable and shared my situation with some trusted peers at work and asked to move the board meeting, but I didn't. Shouldering the secret alone, I took a vacation day to have the egg-extraction procedure. There was no soul tribe around me, but I wished for one and desperately needed one.

Part of a woman's authentic journey in life involves addressing her fertility: yes, no, maybe, wait, pause, urgent. We don't get a hall pass from this experience and we must face the questions and honour our own individual answers or find peace with the answers served to us by our greater destiny. Regardless, we all need to lean into a tribe of women – perhaps a different tribe from our regular tribe – that can support us through this major transition.

Melinda echoed my own experience of needing a soul tribe: 'Everyone is at a stage where they are having babies and you seem to be the only one who isn't. You sit in this room with this diversity of ages and backgrounds. You think: "Oh, gosh, it is not just me." I have seen it really powerfully shift people's minds. These trials, worries, concerns and fears – it is not only me.'

The power of the tribe heals. Another woman's story may express the anger that is suppressed rage beneath our own surface we have forgotten until we are reminded through storytelling. The story gives us permission to feel the anger, and in that moment we are validated and supported. This is the chance for the anger to be understood, released and transmuted. Another woman may have access to the tears we can't access ourselves. We may have been weighed down by the burden of needing to be a certain way: perfect, stoic, dry faced. In a soul tribe circle, women can be the vehicle to access the emotions in each other. These shared stories are gateways to our release and to understanding our emotions.

The tribe we need around is not just about fertility or infertility. When we are going through a difficult stage in our Courageous Path we need to seek and look for those who are going through the same experiences.

You will need to seek out new soul tribes to support you at different stages of your Courageous Path.

Melinda said, 'There are at least a couple of women who don't talk, and they are the ones who email me and say, "Even though I am not talking, I absolutely love and appreciate this conversation. It is really affecting me and helping me." In groups, there are always a couple of women who talk, who are happy to share. It is about normalising the situation so we don't feel we are so alone. It allows us to talk about things we feel are taboo on this journey. By talking about it and sharing it and speaking about our experiences, we realise our own wisdom.

'Storytelling normalises our experience. People feel they can talk about the dark stuff, about messy, difficult and complicated stuff. There is such empathy and everyone feels it. It is the freedom to finally be able to talk about things in an environment where people get it and there is no judgement. As each person shares their story, people nod their heads, they will make noises, you can see the validation around the room.'

Your soul tribe of emotional support is critical on your Courageous Path. You will mirror back parallel life stories, your tragedies and triumphs. You may be at different stages of the healing process, but you will cause a surge in the healing of others and, in turn, will receive the healing you need from the stories shared with you.

AMY: BEING WITNESSED IN A VIRTUAL SPACE

Genuine sisterhood is more than merely supporting others through our words or mutual interest; rather it is measured by our ability to stay there at the raw, messy depths. Through the hurricanes, the floods and the fires. Genuine sisterhood is a powerful force.

REBECCA CAMPBELL

Remember my friend Amy who was working as the editor for Doreen Virtue's column *My Guardian Angel*? She listened, read and witnessed women's angel stories every week, then when the stories were published the invisible sacred circle was established. Some women needed their angel stories witnessed and some women needed to witness angel stories. It is not surprising that after editing the column for several years Amy felt a bigger pull to start running a women's circle of her own: a virtual online circle.

She told me: 'The most common pattern I see in circles is women who are ready to come out of hiding. Women who are ready to be witnessed, ready to show up in full radiance but who need support. Women hide. Women hide from our power. I include myself. Unfolding and empowerment work can take years. It took years to get hidden. So it can take years to unhide.

'Online groups give us a way of connecting with women we might not be able to find in our offline world. Everyone acknowledges that virtual reality allows people to experiment with identity, to select the information and the qualities of self we choose to share. Virtual space is imaginative, liminal, infinitely expansive. In my circles we use that flexibility to experiment with new ways of relating, new ways of supporting others. We develop friendships, even attract fans and supporters to our own work. In a good online group where there are gatekeepers moderating the conversation we can feel safe to allow the invisible parts of ourselves to become visible. We can echo into view. We can feel how it feels to be seen. We can get used to it in our safe online group, and then the challenge is to translate these visibility skills into offline life. In other words, how might we emerge in full radiance in our real lives?'

You will be seen by your soul tribe.

Amy explained the real reason she loved running online groups was because the virtual space offered women safety: 'The women in a closed virtual group will know why you are there. In my groups we know you are there for soul work. So I think it feels safer to talk about parts of ourselves and our lives we may normally veil. As other women speak honestly about their confusion and fear and share stories about their marriages, their teenage kids, their work and financial concerns, it may help us feel safer to share our own experiences. You see that you are not going to get hurt here. In fact, you are going to be supported. So what I witnessed as my groups formed was a lot of emotions pouring out.'

Profound shifts can occur in an online community: 'Most importantly, I run global groups that include women from everywhere: Australia, South Korea, Canada, South America, South Africa, not just the USA. So there is this experience of a woman having a breakdown online and someone online is awake around the world. Someone is witnessing them because of this global community.

'A woman would post "I just had a fight with my husband!" and immediately another woman would respond "I see you." Then another comment appeared: "Breathe." A moment later: "I'm here, too, breathing with you." It was beautiful. There was this witnessing. It wasn't fixing; it was a feeling of "I am here holding you."

'Circle sisters would wake up at different times around the world and you would get this echo effect. So, for example, Debbie in California is being held by women around the world. That evening someone in Australia wakes up and holds her again, so there is this amazing echo quality about the global community.

'We need to be able to witness and be witnessed as the path into deeper authenticity is messy and complicated and the inner struggle is real. Sometimes we need to seek a safe environment to unhide ourselves, and these new groups help us to address our outcast self, the self we have rejected that is now looking for a home. Finding "home" in an online group can be the first step to finding our way home to ourselves.'

LEON: SOUL FAMILY WITH A PURPOSE

Alone we can do so little; together we can do so much.

HELEN KELLER

The book publishing industry is a close-knit community in Australia and sometimes when we meet up it feels like a book club. Perhaps it is also because it is an industry that has so many quirks, secrets, tall tales and short stories. We are respectful friends when working together and sweet rivals when competing in a book manuscript auction, which happens too often. When invited we also attend each other's events if they pique our interest. After one such event I caught up with Leon Nacson, who was facilitating a workshop I was attending.

We had a coffee and I asked him to elaborate on the story he told at the workshop about how he became a publisher after many years in the entertainment industry.

'Did you really run two nightclubs called The African Queen?' I asked. Everyone has a past, I thought as I smiled, knowing this story was going to be interesting. One of Leon's nightclubs had been located in Double Bay, which was to Sydney in the 1980s what Beverly Hills is to California.

'At my nightclub,' he told me, 'I had the Commodores and the Pointer Sisters perform. Up until this point I had never seen a self-help book. I wasn't even familiar with the word "self-help".'

I sat back and stared at Leon, stunned. I could not make the mental leap between managing a nightclub to managing a major iconic publishing house years later.

Leon went on to explain how back in the early 1980's he went to a well-being seminar that focused on tissue cleansing. During the course of this workshop one of the guest speakers was Stuart Wilde: 'I really enjoyed his presentation and asked him if he ever thought about doing this to a large audience and that I would like to promote him.'

Running a successful nightclub in Sydney, Leon knew a lot about promotions: 'At Stuart's first event in Australia I managed to get one thousand people to turn up at the Town Hall in Sydney to hear him speak. Later, when Stuart went back to America, he started to sing my praises to Louise Hay and Wayne Dyer. So the first time Louise came to Sydney I worked on the public relations and that was nearly thirty-five years ago.'

As Leon was speaking I thought back to Louise Hay's book, *You Can Heal Your Life* and what a profound book it had been for its time. Back then, we did not start our mornings with green juices or Keto diets; back then meditation was for monks draped in orange cloth. It was a different time and for many, including myself, Louise's book was so important in the spiritual awakening process.

'Years later, Louise, Reid Tracey and I set up Hay House in Australia. They sent me containers full of stock all on a handshake. There is always a feeling of family to everything we do.'

I laughed, thinking that while Leon said there was no official contract in place perhaps a soul contract had been agreed to in my opinion.

'The next person who got in touch with me was Deepak Chopra, and later I brought him out to Australia also. In fact, Deepak's first few books were self-published. Deepak and I would carry his boxes of books to the back of the seminar room, and he would sign them one by one.'

The simple and hard-working backstories are sometimes more powerful than the happy-ever-after stories. The happy-ever-after was that Hay House went on to become the largest mind, body and spirit publishers globally and still are today.

As I listened to Leon describe the intricacies of printing and publishing books of known and unknown authors, I understood that he started in a modest way but one that he truly believed in. Humble beginnings are just that: humble. The current bestselling authors were once unknown and on occasion self-published. Louise Hay shipped many books to Australia and there was no guarantee of financial success or even that the public would understand and accept the teachings she had to offer. She was an early pioneer of the spiritual self-help industry.

Louise Hay, Reid Tracy, Wayne Dyer and Deepak Chopra may not have dreamed of the scale of what they were creating 35 years ago; they just rolled up their sleeves and, as I believe, said yes to their soul purpose. They took Courageous Leaps to help their soul tribe in distant countries and they did this because they fiercely believed in their mission.

As I listened to Leon describe his journey to becoming CEO of Hay House in Australia I could see how Louise, Reid and Leon were what I call a *soul family*. The way they worked together was sourced from pure passion, inspiration, humility and dedication. That is what it looks like when a soul family comes to work on something greater than themselves.

We cannot walk our path and manifest our dreams alone. There is a soul family waiting to meet you.

Quite often we cannot complete our purpose in isolation. To walk the Courageous Path you may be called on to believe in the mission of others around you, and they in turn will support yours. After time the two paths or multiple paths will merge and become one. The dream you dreamed will be bigger by virtue of meeting your soul family, and they will have the missing pieces to your soul purpose puzzle.

The beginnings of a soul family coming together may not be glamorous and the mission may not be completely understood. So how do you connect to your soul family? You say yes to an invitation, to a new opportunity that comes your way, if it *feels* right. You move into action and be proactive when you feel moved to start a conversation with a stranger who feels like more than a stranger. You will not know why or where it is leading you but it will feel right. It will feel like an alignment of purpose, skills and vision.

TIFFANY: COURAGE TO FOLLOW OR LEAD

Courage can be contagious.
MICHELLE OBAMA

The First Follower principle suggests that the first person who recognises that someone's unique idea has value and supports them turns that person into a leader. This is based on entrepreneur Derek Sivers' TED talk 'How to Start a Movement'. He illustrates his theory with a brief video from an outdoor concert in which a single man begins to dance outrageously while others around him either ignore his dancing or look on curiously, remaining seated. You can sense the collective discomfort of the festival goers: this guy is dancing so crazily and they are not sure if they want to be dancing alongside him. There is also a big part of the crowd that is envious of his inner freedom and his reckless abandon. They do want to join him but they don't know how to. What he is proposing they do is a little too far out for many of them, much like the vision of many movements.

The first person who starts the crazy dancing is the 'initiator'. After a brief period the person who starts dancing next is called the 'first follower'. The first follower risks ridicule in the same way that the initiator does: both have stuck out their proverbial necks for something they believe in. Once a single person follows the initiator it becomes less risky for others to join in, so eventually a third person follows, then a fourth, then a fifth, and the momentum quickly builds. Over time, as enough people join, it actually becomes riskier to stay on the sidelines than to become part of the movement, because now a mass has joined the crazy guy dancing and many have bought into his vision.

Sivers says: 'The first follower is the one who turns someone from a shirtless nut into a leader. The leader will get the credit, but the followers are brave for getting it started.'

My friend Tiffany had always been a visionary thinker. We met at the peak of our corporate careers and our big visions were channelled into our jobs. One day Tiffany packed up her bag and relocated to America on a soul mission. When she founded Sister Suppers there was no template or structure for her grand vision. Her passion was 'women inspiring women'.

Sister Suppers is a movement of women creating community from within their homes. The Sister Suppers platform invites you to either be a dedicated host of a women's circle within your local geographic community or attend a supper in your local area. The rules for hosts are simple: open your home, create a home-cooked meal and facilitate a sharing circle. The logistics are also simple; however, a woman's connection to her sisterhood is complex, necessary and ever growing. Tiffany did not know about the first follower principle, although it was an important concept that helped her create her movement and more importantly enrich the lives of countless numbers of women globally.

Tiffany was not a shirtless nut; she was a woman who believed in her cause. When we believe in a cause greater than ourselves or step in to create something never created before we can sometimes be seen as crazy, irrational, a dreamer or a shirtless nut.

'The women who started Sister Suppers with me are all still hosts, and they keep showing up to the monthly calls. Sister Suppers is not mine. It is like a communal birth. I haven't birthed it; the women birthed it with me.' The Sister Supper hosts are Tiffany's first followers and were inspired by her vision, mission and conviction.

Being a first follower is not all about sacrifice and service. A first follower is rewarded for their courage: 'You know, fellow Sister Supper hosts would say, "Oh, my God, I didn't know that this was what was missing from my life." They would say to me that they felt so much lighter now or that they released something they hadn't ever shared before, or that they got some advice they really needed to hear. The biggest thing I have heard from my hosts is: "I am powerful and you showed me that. You also showed me that I am not alone."'

We are in a time when women are waking up from a long, deep slumber into powerful female to female connections. More than ever before women are inspiring women. There is room for more circles, there is room for the circles to get bigger and there is room for different types of circles. There is more space in our day for collaborations.

Tiffany described what happens when women come together: 'They remember their real essence, strength and power. When woman are in sisterhood together they remember how wise they are. When they are giving other women advice and support they remember how strong they are. When a woman is sitting across from them or in the circle and is in her most vulnerable state she sees herself in the other women. She remembers how powerful we are when we do this work together. When we are not in that place the old paradigm of competition takes over, where there is not enough for everyone, where we think she is better than me.'

At times on your courageous journey you will lead and at times you will step up and be the first follower to support another sister on her journey. Sometimes you will be a smiling face in the crowd cheering on another woman as she steps onto her Courageous Path.

Sivers explains: '. . . as a leader you must encourage your first followers. Embrace them as equals and treat them well . . . If you see a single person with a good idea, be that first follower.'

On your path to deeper authenticity you may be called to start a movement or feel the pull to be in one. Know that changing your life involves changing the world around you and you will need the early support of a couple of fellow women to see your vision.

Tiffany said: 'When I was younger I was told that you can only count the women you can trust, the women who are your friends, on one hand. That is not true. That is not my experience. The more women you have in your life the more supported you feel. I went to do a workshop and I could feel a resistance to make new friends. I stopped myself and thought: why am I capping the number of female friends I have? We are not trained to be abundant in relationships.'

We need to change the mantras about sisterhood. Tiffany's Sister Supper community is now over 20,000 women strong in five countries and growing steadily.

Starting and following a new movement requires great courage.

CLASHES AND CONNECTIONS

Naturally, the antidote to shame is to risk showing up as fully as we're able. The discipline needed for shame is to practice revealing yourself. It is bringing into the open the full brightness of your spirit despite your fear of failure.

TOKO-PA TURNER

Sometimes our new soul tribe will challenge, trigger and ask for a greater part of ourselves to step forward, which can be uncomfortable and cause conflict to arise. I arrived at an ashram in Uttar Pradesh, one of India's poorest states, early in my spiritual path. I was on another fact-finding, soul-searching and hard-core meditation mission and had booked ahead for a 10-day meditation pilgrimage in the heart chakra of India. Enlightenment was on the agenda. When I walked through the gates of the ashram I left the dust and poverty behind and entered a spiritually rich sanctum of like-minded people.

On the very first night things went a little south. My hair is curly and untamed, and straightening it was a daily ritual at home. I was drying my wet hair with a hair dryer and the electric cord kept slipping out of the socket and short circuiting; sparks were flying. I am a determined person, so straightening my mane was going to happen regardless of the voltage, time zone or GDP status of the country I was in. My roommate chimed in with: 'I have never seen anyone in an ashram use a hairdryer before!' Shame and irritation quickly set in. Inwardly I thought: 'Just because we are in an ashram does not mean we let ourselves go.' Outwardly I said in as upbeat a manner as I could: 'Well, there's a first time for everything.'

I made myself very wrong so many times during my stay. My roommate's judgement turned inward to my own self-judgement: I was not pious enough, not spiritual enough, not devoted enough, not vegetarian enough. When I reflect on the experience I can see there was support from the greater tribe I had not acknowledged. One day as I was walking down the street my sari started to unravel because I had not tied it properly, and three women quickly gathered around me to help me to tie it back up. I ran in late to one of the Vedic philosophy lectures and a group of women all parted to make sure I had a seat at the front.

Sometimes on our Courageous Path we need to step into a new soul tribe and not all of the individual connections will be easy; we may feel as though we don't fit in. The larger soul tribe will support you, but you may experience conflict on an individual level. Many times we are being shown aspects of ourselves we need to work on; for me that was patience, tolerance and self-acceptance. Perhaps my roommate was also working on this.

Like my sari I needed to unravel, and the women who rescued me from embarrassment indicated I was being supported by a larger collective soul tribe when I needed it.

Within our new soul tribes, look at every experience as an ability to love, grow and heal.

CAROL: SOUL MUMS

I believe the choice to become a mother is the choice to become one of the greatest spiritual teachers there is.

OPRAH WINFREY

Sometimes other people's mums can become your mum on your soul journey. Soul mums are different from soul sisters within your soul tribe: they are way more at ease with themselves and are ahead of you on the Courageous Path, which is why you are drawn to them. The blessed hand of ageing has removed their anxiety and self-consciousness. When I have sat with these women they have put me at ease. When they say to me 'It will all be okay, don't worry,' it is in those moments I believe them and the anxiety sitting in my body dissolves. I trust their words.

We all need multiple soul mothers. They are the mothers your soul's evolution needs and you can manifest them. The wisdom from a soul mother will feel as though an ascended mistress is sitting in a downtown café having a turmeric latte with you. The exchange will be equal. I know my zeal, utterly blind optimism and naïve get-up-and-go has also invigorated my soul mothers' spirits.

The moment of meeting tends to be later in life when we have found a level of peace and acceptance or are in a process of deep inquiry into our own family of origin and the incongruence we may feel around this. Perhaps you can't speak to your own mother, or your mother or grandmother may have left the physical plane. We need maternal, meaningful, mature support on our Courageous Path, but our own soul may not be able to heal and expand without it. Just as with a fairy godmother, soul mums show up.

I met Carol, one of my soul mothers, when I joined a beginner's psychic development circle. We shared our battle scars through the sacred art of storytelling at an afternoon brunch.

'I was a volunteer at the hospital after my cancer,' Carol began. 'I wanted to give back to a community that had helped me. After my voluntary shift at the hospital they would have these free meditation sessions. It was packed with people: up to fifty. I would walk in and no one would say "Hello, who are you, what's your name?" I could slip in there unnoticed. I could go into this meditative state with all these other conscious beings.'

'Why did you like being unnoticed?' I asked.

'I don't know why, but we feel we have to be so identified with what we do, who we are and where we come from. I was tired of people asking me that. "Who are you married to? How many kids do you have?" I didn't want to be identified with that any more; I just wanted to be me. At that time in meditation I could just be me. People would look at me and smile. There was this outpouring of love.'

I had felt the same way. When I went to the psychic development circle no one asked what job I had or where I was from. It was as though everyone in the circle knew those were not the questions to ask and knew that being with each other was more important. I was unaware that I was part of a sacred circle in those beginner days, as it felt more like a refuge circle. We were a group of women who didn't feel as though we had a home; rather, we felt displaced with these spiritual experiences and abilities and with having no one else to share them with. Those friendships started so much more slowly than some of my other friendships but felt so much deeper over time. It was like I was being seen for the first time in my life, possibly because I was seeing myself for the first time. I was looking in a mirror and honestly allowing the job title, the suburb I lived in and all the adornments to fall away. I was undecorated and naked and discovering authenticity for the first time in my life. My smile held the lifetime of who I was. When I smiled at my new friends, my soul tribe, they saw who I was. Carol was one of those friends, a soul mum. She didn't say much in those early days, but every time she did say something it was sage advice. I listened keenly, silently drinking from her full cup of wisdom as she spoke.

Soul mums have travelled further on their Courageous Path.
Their wisdom shared with us becomes our wisdom.

SOUL MENTORS

A mentor is someone who sees more talent and ability within you than you see in yourself and helps bring it out of you.

BOB PROCTOR

Sometimes you will walk on treacherous unchartered terrain on your Courageous Path, forging new trails and facing changeable weather, and a soul mentor is critical. They can show you how to navigate the path and ensure you do not take unnecessary detours or get lost. When the inner teacher is ready the outer mentor will emerge. Yes: the teacher resides within *you* and a conscious mentor will reveal this to you by asking reflective, revealing and sometimes challenging questions.

A week after I lost my job – the job where after the interview my handbag snapped – I descended into depression. I was bang in the middle of another awakening. 'Does the awakening ever end?' I asked myself as I sat in a sunlit café in Sydney with my head in my hands. 'Is there a beginning, middle and end to this process?' I felt overwhelming despair and knew I needed support.

Back then I was painfully aware I was transitioning out of my corporate career, yet I had no idea how to manage this big change. I scrolled through my phone and wrote a list of all the people I knew who might be able to help me in some way. There was no fixed agenda: I called each person and arranged to meet them for coffee. I was sending out an SOS flare to the universe, asking for help.

The universe always listens and answers your deepest heart's desires. A week later my next soul mentor appeared. She was instructional, knowledgeable and practical and I soaked up her wisdom weekly. She held my hand as though I was a child learning to walk for the first time and she guided me through the initial stages of working professionally as a medium.

A soul mentor may propel you exponentially in a new direction; they can be the pattern interruption that is needed on your Courageous Path. My second mentor, a spiritual teacher I admired, lifted me into becoming a spiritual teacher myself. In one of our mentoring sessions she said: 'You are ready.' How potent those three words were to me! Your soul mentors lead by example and will help you amplify the virtues needed on your Courageous Path: integrity, generosity, compassion, empathy and self-awareness. They will embody these qualities themselves and provide great wisdom.

You are called to seek a soul mentor.

A soul mentor relationship is rarely without a disruption: you will go through multiple breakdowns in the process of inner change. Your mentor will hold the crucible that you sit in during this process as you experience the death of the old version of yourself. This will be uncomfortable yet familiar ground for your soul mentor, so they will be able to show you the way.

I have had great mentors in my life who have all showed me how to slow down and be patient when I was rushing, how to take my Courageous Leaps. They encouraged me to work hard when apathy set it, and showed me how to celebrate my achievements when my perfectionist self cast shadows of doubt. They gave me optimism when I was lost and realism when I was ungrounded. Ultimately your soul mentor will teach you to connect to yourself. They will show you the way to take your greatest wound and turn it into your greatest superpower.

Mentoring can be cyclical, and you may return to your soul mentor after a break. The medicine may have been too strong initially so you may have needed to press the pause button on the relationship and integrate the learning. When you are ready for the next steps on your Courageous Path you can reach out for them again, or you may reach for another soul mentor. A mentor on the Courageous Path can show you the way when you are lost and walking the path alone becomes too difficult. You will always be guided by a strong, firm hand if you choose one.

SARAH: STEPPING FORWARD

For those who believe, no proof is necessary. For those who don't believe, no proof is possible.

STUART CHASE

You will never know when you will be called on to mentor others or where your gifts will guide you to helping others on their Courageous Paths. Over the years of working as a medium I knew I was doing more than bridging the physical and spiritual worlds. I knew I was healing people through their grief, educating them about the greater virtues in life and showing them how to forgive. Many times I was able to help clients recognise their own spiritual gifts and greater purpose.

Sarah came up to me at the end of a two-day spiritual workshop I was running to say she was stuck in her life and to request a private reading. I'd pretty much packed up but I agreed, and we found a quiet corner to sit in. It took a few minutes for me to still myself and connect with the energy of spirit. The messages started coming through.

I could see clear visions of a broom sweeping, so I asked: 'Do the words "broom", "sweeping" or "sweep" mean anything to you?' She was silent for a short time before saying: 'Sweep was the name of our family cat when I was a child.'

I love readings where the communication is strong and I can feel the spirit close to me. With this confirmation I focused again and heard the word 'mother' come strongly in my inner ear. I shared with Sarah gently: 'I have your mother here and she wants to speak to you about your life and help give you direction.'

Sarah's jaw dropped. She looked at me and broke into tears, saying: 'I lost my mother at a very young age.'

I took a deep breath. It does not matter how many times I do mediumship readings for clients: I am always moved by those who have had to experience loss early in their lives. I know they have chosen a courageous life.

Over the next 30 minutes Sarah's mother shared memories and messages of love. She also was insistent about giving Sarah guidance on her life and how to step forward. By the end of the reading it was clear that Sarah knew she had spiritual gifts but needed time to process the information about how to move forward with them. She had always doubted her abilities, but her mother in spirit found the exact words needed to help Sarah overcome this doubt. 'Just believe in yourself' were the words I heard in my ear, and I relayed them to Sarah. The look on Sarah's face showed it wasn't just the words, it was who they had come from that mattered.

Six months later Sarah contacted me: 'That reading you did for me had a profound effect. I've been doing a lot of thinking and journal writing and I feel like I'm now ready to develop my intuitive abilities further. I'm feeling it's my path to work in this field. Will you mentor me?'

I could see myself in Sarah and reflected on my own path: I had also had doubts about my intuitive abilities. While we walk the path to serve ourselves, we find that in the process we also serve others. The challenges we face on our Courageous Path transmute into gifts we can offer to others. The feelings of great satisfaction in being able to be a soul mentor for Sarah confirmed, once again, the value of walking my own path.

You will be a soul mentor for those who are walking a similar
Courageous Path to yourself.

COURAGEOUS TRUTHS

1. You must be honest with yourself about whether your current soul tribes are aligned with your Courageous Path.
2. You may need a new soul tribe to support you during a particular challenging experience or transition into a new area of interest in your life.
3. You will be *seen* by your soul tribe, which is how you will know they are your tribe.
4. You may be called to collaborate with members of your soul tribe, which is why you have been brought together. You are *soul family*.

5. Your soul tribe may mirror the ways you need to grow and heal. Be open to these lessons and how they serve your path.

6. Soul mums will nurture you on your path and share with you the wisdom your soul needs.

7. Soul mentors are essential for navigating new experiences and difficult transitions in your life.

8. The people you are looking to have soul connections with are also looking for you.

GET CURIOUS QUESTIONS

1. Which friends or soul tribes support you to feel powerful, inspired and aligned to your path?

2. Do you feel completely nourished by the current tribes you spend time with?

3. Do you feel guilty about letting go of relationships that rely on you or no longer serve you? What are you afraid of losing if you let them go?

4. Are you going through a challenging time or a transition? Do you have a soul tribe around you to support you right now?

5. Is there already a soul tribe that needs your support and wisdom?

6. Do you have a soul tribe around you to help you with your dream, calling, purpose or creative projects? If not, where could you find them?

7. Do you have a tribe of older women to guide you or can you seek one?

8. What fears and concerns do you have about seeking out your tribe?

9. Do you have a soul mentor assisting you on your Courageous Path or can you seek one?

POWER PHRASE

'The soul tribes in my life provide love, support, knowledge and wisdom in abundance and I provide this in return.'

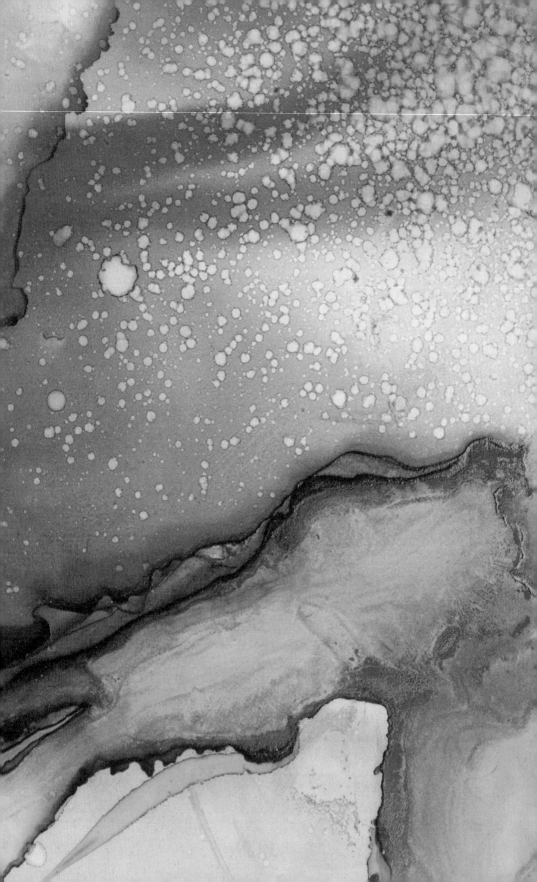

CHAPTER 6

The courage to wander

Travel not to find yourself but to remember
who you have been all along.

– ANONYMOUS

ALLOWING YOURSELF TO ROAM

We will feel a magnetic pull to be guided where we are meant to go; the pilgrimage is a rite of passage on the Courageous Path. We know that our current life, environment and routines cannot facilitate the changes we are seeking and the pilgrimage is essential to expedite the shift required to discover new possibilities and a fresh way forward. The pilgrimage can serve as the bridge for this, and we may need to get lost before we can be found.

On your pilgrimage you will be running away from something and towards something in equal proportions. This is okay, but notice what you need, want and desire to leave behind. What are you reaching for? What is feeling unfulfilled in your life that you need to search for: a loveless marriage, a rewarding career at the cost of burnout and family, three perfect children and relentless utter exhaustion? Do you dare to reach for more meaning in your good but not great life? What transformation are you yearning for? What within you is lost that needs to be found?

We delay pilgrimages for many reasons, and when we delay the pilgrimage we delay a transformation that is essential for our personal growth. We are delaying the necessary, so we allow excuses and delaying tactics to set in. We question whether we are worthy enough to take ourselves out of our routine, a routine where other people rely on us. Can we go to a faraway place that makes no sense to the people in our lives? We must give ourselves permission to go.

A courageous act is giving yourself permission to go.

BARBARA: GIVING YOURSELF PERMISSION

Oh, the places you'll go!

DR SEUSS

I met Barbara many years ago at my first women's circle. We were spiritually hungry and open for a soulful friendship. Over a marathon story-swapping session with Barbara I asked her: 'How did your husband let you go away to a retreat in Bali for ten days, leaving him with two young kids?'

Barbara said, 'He was awesome: fully supportive all along. Initially *I* actually stood in my way. I asked him without full conviction or commitment, so it was like I didn't want to go myself. Mother's guilt. I didn't book. I just decided not to go, even though I really wanted to.'

Barbara's delaying tactic sounded like self-sabotage; I understood the feeling well. I didn't have a husband but I had a boss, a work husband, and it felt at times as though the job wouldn't function without me at the helm – or so I indulgently thought. There was always a deadline that kept me stuck.

Barbara continued, 'My father passed away and it was a really tough time as I got closer to the time of the Bali trip. Then I thought to myself: who am I *not* to do this? Yes, I am going for ten days and no, I am not going to feel guilty about going. I booked the flights that day.'

As Barbara shared her thought processes I could feel how much strength it would have taken to allow herself this brief reprieve from the responsibility of a young family, feeling financially selfish and shifting the enormous weight of a mother's guilt. I also thought about how much she actually needed to go, as the trip was the medicine and healing she required.

We sat in silence, and I smiled as I watched Barbara travel back in her memory to that time she spent in Bali. She said: 'I have this wild dream, Sheila, about changing the landscape of parenting.'

In that moment I knew she would succeed.

The Courageous Leap to go on the pilgrimage was the lesson: ironically, we must learn and first overcome that which we will teach others later. What came after was an added bonus for Barbara, who now teaches mindfulness to mothers. The act of going on the pilgrimage taught her an important lesson, one that she will impart to those who cross her path. She has the lived experienced of asking herself the question 'Who am I *not* to do this?' and then powerfully answering the question.

Sometimes the lessons of the pilgrimage are taught well before you leave.

EPIPHANIES AND PLAIN TRUTHS

If you travel far enough, one day you will recognise yourself coming down the road to meet you. And you will say – yes.

MARION WOODMAN

A sense of belonging isn't a place; it doesn't exist outside yourself. I felt a piece of me was missing but I didn't quite know what it was. I had travelled the world but never to my own country of origin: maybe that was where I would find the missing piece of myself? I am an Australian–born Sri Lankan and felt a confusing mix of cultures. I was black on the outside but felt different on the inside, more connected to a Western culture than the culture of my birth.

Sri Lanka is a country with a history of conflict, of civil war, but maybe I could find a foundation, an essence of myself, to heal the conflict I was feeling within. I was doing my MBA and felt I no longer belonged in my social circle, a tight-knit group of girls I had known since my early years at university. Where did I belong?

I was 34, single and committed to my corporate career. Most of my friends had become wives and mothers and were following different paths. I felt the gap between us widening, the common ground between us shifting. I was a lone wolf who had chosen an unconventional life, and wasn't able to articulate how isolated I felt. To face up to this isolation I would have to admit I needed to make major changes in my life, to recalibrate how out of place I was. I needed to accept that I was different, which was okay. A part of me wanted to stay with the pack while another part yearned for a sense of belonging.

I backpacked through the exotic and unfamiliar land of Sri Lanka for three weeks. I looked into the faces of the locals and saw reflected to me my own dark brown eyes, toothy smile and plump cheeks. Despite physically looking like everyone else, the reality was that I was a Sri Lankan woman who had lived all her life in Australia. In Australia it was my appearance that made me feel different at times, but in Sri Lanka I was still seen as an outsider.

Raised with Western values, I did not think it odd to be travelling alone with a backpack on my back. Many locals asked questions such as: 'Where is your husband?' and 'Did your father let you travel alone?' These questions highlighted the fact I didn't fully belong in Sri Lanka, that this was not my home even though part of me longed to feel as though it was. Changes were needed in my life.

When I returned to Australia I knew I had personal development work to do, and realised that belonging meant accepting all the disowned parts of my life. The epiphany was that I had gone a long distance to find myself even though I had been there the entire time. The pilgrimage gave me the experience that it wasn't a place, that it was something I had to find within myself. This was not the truth I was looking for, but that is how truths work: they are waiting in plain sight to be discovered, sometimes in a foreign land.

A pilgrimage may take you home to yourself.

YOU MUST BE READY

We go into a relationship looking for love, not realising that we must bring love with us.
IYANLA VANZANT

Pilgrimages are rarely a last-minute escape. Essentially a seed is planted, an idea or a destination niggles away at you, and eventually you can't refuse the calling any longer. It may be to Bodh Gaya in India to plant yourself down where Buddha sat, or you may be drawn to flip your downward dog in Bali. You must wait for the seed to germinate, and when it does you will feel ready to go. The timing is important, because if you go before things feel right for you then you might not be completely ready for the nudge to your soul. If you go when your soul is still young and green like a baby coconut you may be cracked open in a way that is not transformative.

'You want to go to the Amazon?' my family and friends asked, intrigued. 'What is there in the Amazon for you? It is a dangerous place.' I didn't know where to start with justifying where I was going or what I was doing, so I didn't; I felt the conversation had to end there. How could I explain it was a trip my soul was yearning for? At some level the future was already present with me: there was a knowing of the lasting benefits and healing I would experience. I couldn't find the words to make sense of it, but I knew I was ready to go.

For some pilgrimages you must be ready.

I was in the middle of the Amazon jungle perspiring heavily. A part of me could not believe I was actually experiencing this sacred psychedelic ritual of drinking ayahuasca, a brew made from an Amazonian vine and leaf with powerful hallucinogenic properties that claim to open your mind and heal past traumas.

Two months prior to going I had ended a significant relationship and was again at a crossroad in my career and life. I was at the end of my rope and had experienced every modality of therapy to deal with my limiting self-beliefs and low self-worth. I was sick and tired of the same old relationships showing up in my life in which it wouldn't take long for me to become excessively insecure and co-dependent. This recurring storyline had to end: I was truly at a loss as to how I had reached the age of 40 and joined the 'unmarried and childless' club. The picture did not make sense.

I had big sexy hair, a magnetic personality and sassy lady bumps, so why was I so unmarriageable, so single? My blind spot was that I hadn't met the right person because *I* wasn't the right person and constantly attracted a string of uncommitted, semi-committed or will-commit-in-the-future men.

When this relationship ended, dark and darker thoughts pervaded my mind. One night I sat alone cross-legged in my apartment and contemplated ending my life. I had never had suicidal thoughts before, but a thought like that only needs to enter your mind once. It was a seed that didn't need to germinate, so three days later I booked my flights to the Amazon.

I was told that drinking one cup of ayahuasca is like doing 10 years of therapy. I had already done many years of therapy and now I wanted to sip from this cup. My heart was racing as I took a big gulp of the foul-tasting and potent elixir. The sludge trickled down the back of my throat; it would take 30 minutes for the effects to kick in. I had to sit back and wait. My heart started to thump.

There is a spiritual protocol when engaging in an ayahuasca ceremony: a strict diet over a four-week period is required, avoiding salt, spices, red meat, alcohol and drugs in the lead up to the ceremony. It is also recommended that you set an intention. Mine was: 'Show me my fears and how they do not serve me. Show me what true love feels like.'

Ayahuasca is commonly known in the Amazon as 'la purge'. Over five ceremonies I projectile vomited, cried uncontrollably, shook furiously and purged my toxic thoughts. I released repeated patterns I was holding on to believing they served me and would keep me safe. I let go of unconscious patterns handed down through my ancestral lines. It was exhausting, illuminating and exhilarating all at the same time.

Ayahuasca put a spotlight on the parts of my life that were holding me back. I was shown the unconditional love offered to me by my family that I had been too stubborn and blind to see. I had been living my life with closed fists and not an open heart. I was shown how my negative, victim mindset had adversely impacted my life, and was shown that I was fearful of living my life as my authentic self. In this psychedelic haze I could not turn away from reality: I had to sit for five hours each night in the great discomfort of my limiting and judgemental thoughts.

The spiritual epiphanies were life changing and the visions were extraordinary. There were visions of the potential of a life lived with no fear. I saw that to bring real love into my life required giving up my staunch independence. I loved my career and feared it would be compromised if I had a relationship in my life, which was not the case. The relationship I was looking for could not be reduced to a checklist; I had to embody all the qualities I was looking for in the partner I wished to attract. During the ceremony I was admonished about daring to believe I was unlovable, especially by my close family and friends. It was not that the love did not exist but that I could not see it or receive it. This was a selfish part of my personality, the rejection of the love of my family and friends.

At the end of the ceremony I was flooded with feelings of unconditional love from my father. Up until this moment I had foolishly felt his love was conditional upon me being a good girl and successful. With this limiting belief I only attracted conditional and demanding love in my romantic relationships. I broke myself to be loved, then the relationship inevitably broke.

Eighteen months later, after returning to Sydney, I attracted a beautiful relationship into my life. It is a true spiritual partnership. We've helped grow each other's souls with love and patience and we both independently do the inner work. Our greater visions are aligned as we are passionate about helping humanity. We are brave and inspire this quality in each other. We are mirrors for each other. When I look at the reflection of this relationship I see my own courage, committed love and ability to be vulnerable and I know that my partner also sees this.

For some pilgrimages you are certain of the transformation.
What you are about to do makes no sense. Go, and do not justify yourself.
You don't need to; your soul knows.

SOUL PILGRIMAGES

We don't receive wisdom; we must discover it for ourselves after a journey that no one can take for us or spare us.
MARCEL PROUST

On our pilgrimage we can become a master storyteller who heals others with our stories as well as healing ourselves. The story of our life changes shape and form and soon we see the strength and courage we have experienced in our story and our lives.

We find meaning in the pain we have experienced. We come to understand that pain that is deeply processed transmutes into strength and resilience, not just for ourselves but for the collective. We are not alone; we are never alone.

On our pilgrimage we may lean into our masters, teachers, mentors, shamans and gurus. They have walked further than we have and we wish to drink from their cups. Over time we also see their humanness, and they reflect our own humanness as they grapple with their own self-worth and continued expansion. Our teachers hold us as we break down and rebuild ourselves. We may project a weaker version of ourselves onto them as we face our uncomfortable truths. The process is messy, but it is meant to be messy.

Forever connections will be made on our pilgrimage. Lifelong soul sister and brother connections will be made as we bond through rituals. On the final day of a retreat we hug each other and hold each other for longer than normal. We are friends for life, not because of the bellyache laughs shared over sips of green tea but because during the tough times where anger, shame and resentment surfaced ungraciously we didn't walk away. We stood strong in ourselves to support others, knowing we would all get to the other side: the side of transformation. This is the elixir for the lifelong friendships that are made when we go on a pilgrimage.

You will connect to your soul tribe on your pilgrimage.

PILGRIMAGES CLOSER TO HOME

They say nothing lasts forever: dreams change, trends come and go, but friendships never go out of style.

CARRIE, SEX AND THE CITY

Sometimes we need familiar company to make ourselves feel safe and hold us while we disappear internally. We don't always need to head to a distant land; we just need to leave the current status quo behind in our mind.

When I resigned from my corporate career I headed up the coast with my best friend. She is blue-eyed and blonde and has a young family: the complete opposite to me. We would joke that we had nothing in common yet everything in common. We certainly had an uncommon bond. After 24 years of friendship we didn't need to justify our connection any more, as our souls knew we were sisters from lifetimes ago.

On this pilgrimage we both needed the luxury of time: no husbands, boyfriends, children or work emails. We gave each other extended periods of undivided attention, a rare commodity. We pressed the reset button an hour's drive from where we lived.

The silence I would lapse into was not questioned; I needed to dive deep to understand the transition I was going through. We vacillated in our discussions about the many layers of our adult lives, such as a marriage that seemed to be great one day and challenging the next. That is marriage, isn't it: sick parents and restless children? Our bond deepened as we sat with each other in each other's pain. We then reminisced about the past: younger bodies and hopeful minds. Laughter punctuated the heaviness in the air. A great friendship can be so pliable and so essential on our pilgrimage, and I needed sage advice from someone who knew my soul.

Problems are universal but the solutions are also universal; it's just the flavours that are different. We assume we are going through problems alone but we are not. Grief through death, recovering from an illness, the shock of a job loss, a marriage that has hit a rough patch, boredom when we seek excitement: sometimes we need to be surrounded by the familiar as we enter the unfamiliar parts of ourselves. On this pilgrimage with my best friend we guided each other through the bumpy terrain of our individual paths; we had a lifetime of memories to draw from. We gave strength and wise guidance to each other. Sometimes this is how a pilgrimage serves.

Some pilgrimages are close to home.

COURAGEOUS TRUTHS

1. A courageous act is giving yourself permission to go on your pilgrimage.
2. You may search for belonging on your pilgrimage and you will find it within yourself.
3. You may be called to a distant land and not know why; your soul remembers.
4. Be ready for the transformation offered to you on your pilgrimage.

5. Become a masterful storyteller on your pilgrimage, as this is the healing you give others and yourself.
6. You do not need to pilgrimage far, as you are seeking to connect with yourself and the loving relationships in your life.

GET CURIOUS QUESTIONS

1. How long has it been since you went on a pilgrimage: too long? Never?
2. What do you need to do to give yourself permission to go on a pilgrimage?
3. What part of the world are you being called to pilgrimage to?
4. Could a pilgrimage help you to heal through grief or loss?
5. Can you start to journal a vision or dream about where you would like to travel to?
6. Can you pilgrimage together with your soul tribe?

POWER PHRASE

'A powerful pilgrimage awaits me.'

CHAPTER 7

Dark Night of Courage

We can allow the pain of adversity to
break us open instead of breaking us down,
making us bitter or closing our hearts.

– ELIZABETH LESSER

THE TRANSFORMATION THAT IS NEEDED

The Courageous Path is not courageous without the darkness. You are only cheating yourself to cherry pick the lighter, safer and more comfortable choices as they are presented to you. The uncomfortable truth is that you will find your way home to your true self through the darkness.

You *will* experience a Dark Night of Courage on your Courageous Path, perhaps more than once. A dark night is a spiritual, emotional and mental initiation that takes you from one stage in your life to another. It is more than a depression; it is a transformational experience. It will appear in your life as a crisis. The journey between some stages on your Courageous Path can only happen through the experience of a dark night; however, only hindsight will show you this.

The tears of sadness, sleepless nights, scary conversations, bright red embarrassment and nervous endings are perhaps the most important stages of the Courageous Path. We feel we are not productive when we are in the dark night: we feel alone, singled out and punished. The days are sluggish, productivity is low and there is lethargy in our ambition. This is the way it is meant to be. We label relationship breakdowns, bankrupt businesses or job losses as failures. There is a direct correlation between how attached we are to our old life and the depth of darkness we need to plunge into. We feel we may be stepping into failure, but the only failure is not living our life our own way. It is during this time of perceived inertia that a great transformation is occurring internally.

Can we give ourselves permission to remain in the darkness, to truly allow our full transformation to occur?

The challenge with the dark night in Western culture is that it doesn't have a sense of value or importance in modern busy lives. Those around us can yank us out of this state too early as the symptoms of a dark night can be inconvenient and uncomfortable for them. Dark nights are anti-social. Goals dissolve, for there is little energy to do much else as our true inner self becomes more understood. We can become too weak to resist and too tired to fight with our thoughts. Our emotions are ready to come to the surface to be released.

Our outlook on life is permanently altered after a dark night; that is its purpose. This is how the dark night serves us. When we meet the dark night with courage we stand to amplify the transformation in our life and fortify our resilience. But this is a choice, as with all things in life. If we let it, our dark night can be a mystical, transformative and profound experience. Once we are awake we can no longer go back to sleep; once we have seen we cannot unsee.

If your life looks messy and you feel like you are going mad then things are perfect. This is your dark night.

PATTERN INTERRUPT

Things do not change, we change.

HENRY DAVID THOREAU

Sometimes our dark night interrupts a repeating pattern. The darkest of nights is when the pattern has repeated so many times we are broken within. We need to stop dating the wounded men we want to heal, stop attracting the bully at work, stop being empty on self-love or stop finding ourselves constantly broken from a lack of boundaries.

The brain is wired to detect patterns. When our patterns are repeated so often this behaviour becomes stored in our unconscious mind. But we see our own patterns as outliers and random events as bad luck that are in no way connected and are definitely not our fault. The dark night interrupts those patterns. When we experience a dark night we think of it as an extraordinary experience, yet it is an exceptionally ordinary experience and no one escapes this fate during their lifetime. We all have patterns in our life that need to be stopped or reduced, and sometimes the Dark Night of Courage is the only circuit breaker or reset button that will allow the pattern to stop.

Can you identify any unhealthy patterns repeating in your life?

RESISTING THE DARK NIGHT

Rule of thumb: The more important a call or action is to our soul's evolution, the more Resistance we will feel toward pursuing it.

STEVEN PRESSFIELD

Resisting the dark night is a common affliction. Why are we so fearful of change when the change assists us in creating the authentic life we seek? At stages on the Courageous Path you may need to question: 'Am I standing in the resistance of necessary change?'

Our resistance can last days, weeks, months, years or a lifetime if we are unconscious of the process. Later we may refer to this time of resistance as a 'waste'. We may say to ourselves: 'Why did I stay in that job when I was so miserable?', 'Why did I stay in that relationship when I knew we were not right for each other?' or 'Why couldn't I just take a baby step forward to starting my own business?' We resist the dark night because we think it takes us off our path when really it propels us along the path we are meant to be on.

In the lead up to a dark night we may experience apathy, which drains energy and leaves us feeling lifeless and irritable. It is a form of resistance. I was waiting for someone or something to bring me happiness but was unaware that I had to make the change myself. It was a time during which I considered myself a victim and blamed many people around me: ex-boyfriends who had left me wounded, bosses who were controlling and demanding, staff who didn't work hard enough. I was tough on those people and even tougher on myself. I was taking out my resentment of living an inauthentic life on those closest to me. I wish someone had tapped me on the shoulder and said: 'Move along now, greatness awaits: a new life better than one you could dream for yourself.'

When I returned from The Arthur Findlay College I knew without any doubt that my calling in life was to work professionally as a medium. The scales had now tipped towards my passion and life purpose. It was time for safety and security to be sacrificed for the future that lay ahead, yet still I resisted making the necessary changes in my life.

I questioned whether a cluster of painful trials in a short space of time was necessary to wake me up, but I had given the universe no choice. I ran from my dark night and thus a darkness set in long before the trials in my life began. I would not let my life be transformed. Meanwhile, on the sidelines, the course correction was building.

When we resist the dark night it feels much worse. When we surrender to the dark night we are allowing the transformation to occur.

Manifesting is the process of repeatedly saying a statement about a future state with a strong belief, feeling and conviction. Quite often we don't realise the power of our internal thoughts and feelings. We *all* have an ability to manifest. I yearned to work as a professional medium, so for 28 days straight I logged on to my computer at work and as the screen warmed up I would say a silent mantra:

'I wish I didn't have this job. I wish I could do my soul work.' I was manifesting. I was unaware that I was also manifesting a series of trials that would allow this wish to come true. I was, in effect, manifesting my dark night.

MY DARK NIGHT

Sometimes when you're in a dark place you think you've been buried, but you've actually been planted.

CHRISTINE CAINE

My life quickly began to disintegrate and disappear. I didn't know I was in the process of being saved from my small life, and during my Dark Night of Courage I felt like a battered and bruised victim.

Dark nights are messy and unglamorous and rarely appear on social media. The first sign for me was when I broke my toe walking: can you believe it! The pain was excruciating. I was not willing to take the next step forward in my life so my body showed me this daily as I looked down at my bandaged, swollen foot. Not being able to move quickly anywhere meant I was forced to slow down and be with my uncomfortable thoughts and emotions, the discomfort of which was encouraging me to change.

Weeks later my apartment flooded. I needed to pack everything up and move out while suffering with a broken toe. New foundations needed to be laid in my property, mirroring a new foundation in my life. I was a woman who never asked for help, but now with an injury I needed to grasp the hands of help that were extended to me. I was forced to consider that I couldn't do life alone.

Then my romantic relationship ended suddenly. I had felt very insecure and it was a distraction from my greater purpose; I was leaking energy into it. 'Am I good enough?' was a daily mantra and it was not serving me at all. I was shown that I needed to address my self-worth issues. Finally, two weeks later, my employer marched me into their office and fired me. I slowly walked the green mile back to my desk as the sounds of the office silenced and all I could hear was a shamanic, thumping drumbeat emanating from my heart. I knew I was about to sink into a journey towards darkness and depression.

How much more could I take?

My resistance was ending. I had not let the dark night completely envelop me but I had opened a door to it. I picked up my crystals from my work desk: black obsidian, clear quartz and rose quartz. I no longer needed protection, clarity and love to get me through my work day. I put these precious rocks carefully into my Michael Kors handbag and walked out.

When nothing makes sense any more you are experiencing a dark night.

A DARK NIGHT IS IMPERATIVE

'You're gonna be happy,' said life, 'but first I'll make you strong.'
CHAVELA VARGAS

My life was not going to be transformed without my dark night. I felt frightened when it was happening as there was no assurance that things would be okay if I chose this new path. My big career goals and aspirations appeared to have been carelessly swept aside by forces beyond my control. The traditional path I was on crumbled and I was cast adrift with no compass, map or light. The days were dark; the weekends were darker. On a Sydney summer's day it was a winter wind that followed me around. In hindsight, even though my life was falling apart it was coming together. Sometimes our life needs to be simplified so we can rebuild it differently. The dark night forced me to stop and consider alternatives even when I believed there were none and that I was stuck.

I was now being *called* to work professionally as a medium. Instead of looking for a new corporate job I paused and used the time between job interviews to create a business website, print business cards and start advertising my services as a professional medium. While internally struggling I was designing and reshaping my life.

The first painful lesson of my dark night was learning how to surrender. There was nothing more to lose as the universe had cleared my life's slate clean. As I transitioned through my dark night the fear eased slowly and I moved towards a state of trust. The dark night was taking me on a journey to become who I was meant to become.

Your life will look different after a dark night. It is meant to.

I was transforming from not living to authentically living. I had been barely surviving. The process required the death of old beliefs that no longer supported me, the death of attachments to materiality and the death of my old identity, then the acceptance of my visions of success and external accomplishments. I grasped with all my might to the old version of myself as the new version had not yet appeared. The new insights, learnings and deeper version of myself had not been fully revealed.

We must allow the dark night to transform us.

MELINDA: THE DARK NIGHT OF A FERTILITY JOURNEY

I learned that when life pulls you under, you can kick against the bottom, break the surface and breathe again.

SHERYL SANDBERG

When we share survival stories of our dark nights with soul sisters, our stories will match in intensity and our shared dark pits of despair will illuminate each other. My friend Melinda recalls the number of invasive treatments she kept going through to fall pregnant before her IVF doctor told her she wouldn't become a mother. This was Melinda's dark night, and she took time off to grieve and question everything: her purpose and her desire to have a child. The dark night forced Melinda to consider her alternatives.

'I left my executive role at an advertising agency. I was burnt out and exhausted and I went on to become a yoga instructor. When I became a teacher I was teaching seventeen classes a week and half of them were in a heated yoga room. When I first started being a yoga teacher I actually burnt out. Okay: so, do you think I had learned the lesson?

'I took nine months off and really grieved. I remember thinking "Is this how it is going to be?" I didn't know the answer, but I thought "I am going to do this and I am going to do this differently." Sometimes you have to come to a place where you say "My life isn't working as I would wish for it; I am going to change and I'm going to try and do it differently."'

Melinda knew there were two possibilities: a life without a child or a year during which she approached her fertility journey without pushing. Surrender and deep, long breaths were what was needed. She thought she was trying to birth a child but what she was really birthing was a new version of herself.

'A friend of mine called me out of the blue. I hadn't spoken to her for ages and she told me that she had had a little girl. Over the phone she recalled to me every push, every strain and the miracle of childbirth without pain relief. I didn't say much on the phone call. I remember putting down the phone and picking up this pillow and screaming into it, absolutely screaming into it. I put it down and I thought, "God, that felt good!"

'So I started to use sound. I would stand facing the wall with my hands pressed on the wall above my head and I would start to breathe deeply. Then I'd start to moan and then it would turn into a groan and then I'd start to cry. It would become a scream and I would just lean into my hands and use sound to get this out of me.'

Sometimes there is a scream in us that we suppress for a long time and we need to let it out, as it hurts us when we don't. Tight lipped, submissive and compliant, we need to yell and scream out the pain. Screaming or sobbing into a dark night is critical.

After losing my corporate job I collapsed, still wearing my suit, on my living room floor. I sobbed from a deep place of shame and cried out to the universe that I believed had forgotten me. I wailed in anger, as I knew I had abandoned myself by working long exhausting hours as an act of service.

The dark night serves to remove our attachment to things. For Melinda it was a child, while for me it was a job title. Even though over-attachment is unhealthy we don't see it. The attachment means we have lost the connection to the truthful part of ourselves. We don't feel that society will accept us or that we could even accept ourselves without the child, the job title, the plus one in our lives. The dark night reconnects us to a part of ourselves that knows we are perfect and that nothing about us needs to change, and until this connection happens life is chaotic and we feel we will be lost forever, an outcast in society. We want to know and have certainty, yet the process of the dark night can be maddening. We are taken to a precipice where uncertainty meets surrender: we let the child go, we let the ex-boyfriends evaporate, the hope of the marriage dissolve, the job titles disintegrate. We hold on to everything in our life a little less tightly, which allows us to move through the dark night and make it to the other side, to the light. The dark night starts a process that enriches our life in other ways, a process of detachment from the thing we so desperately desire.

Do you need to scream, wail and cry? When was the last time you cried?
Crying is a purge; it is not a sign of weakness. It shows you the changes you
need to make.

KATE'S DARK NIGHT

Create your support system before crisis comes.

DANIELLE LAPORTE

When it is dark we cannot see. We cannot see the truth of the changes we need to make in our life. We need to reach out to a friend who has been through their own dark night.

My friend Kate, the policewoman who wanted to change the face of post-traumatic stress in the police force, returned from her first responder training program in Chicago only to face her own burnout and anxiety. Answering her calling, Kate was in the process of opening a yoga studio and spoke of nothing else. Originally she had thought she could offer yoga training at the police academy in their rehabilitation programs, which she saw as an elegant solution to her inner conflict. She wouldn't need to make the major changes in her life she was being called to make. Just because we find a practical solution to our inner conflict does not mean the dark night is over. It might mean that we placate our soul yearnings temporarily, but our soul hunger still remains.

Kate's skills as a policewoman needed to serve in a different way. Training others in yoga was a step on the path, yet the dark night would show her that her practice would be self-care for herself first and then for others later.

Sometimes courage involves swimming upstream against the current, but do we have the stamina? I reflected on my first leap – studying mediumship overseas – and on my subsequent submission back to an ordinary way of life as I did not consider mediumship to be a valid and acceptable full-time vocation. I worked as both a professional medium and corporate executive for three years and I was on the road to burnout. I thought I could hold on to the sparkly corporate title and that my soul cup was being partially filled, but my inner knowing was that it was enough for now. There would be another dark night later when I was called to make another leap into the unknown.

The Courageous Path calls for constant pivots to honour the changes that lead to an authentic life. This agility to make and accept the changes is born from the multiple dark nights we may need to experience. Life for Kate felt like boot camp, and the doors of opportunity were not opening with ease at her work. One morning she went to work and, as she had done so many times before, punched in her security code.

'On this particular morning I couldn't remember my code to enter the precinct. I was embarrassed because I couldn't ask anyone what the code was because it was in my long-term memory. Overnight I stopped remembering simple tasks.' It was the last sign Kate needed to move on: the actual front door to her employment in the Australian police force would not open. Symbolically or literally, she knew it was time to leave.

When we are about to enter darkness we need to reach out to someone who has already emerged from their dark into the light. They are not teachers, but way showers. They offer reassurance, as they have survived their own dark nights. There was a knowing Kate had that she was about to enter into a dark phase, and that I had recently been through my own. Instinctively Kate reached out to me for help.

Sometimes you need every door to shut in your face before you know to stop knocking. I didn't have to support Kate entirely during her dark night, as synchronicity and a stranger did. Before she walked into her sergeant's office to hand in her resignation after nine years of working with the police force, her phone rang.

'Hi, my name is Sophie and I am on the mind/body app trying to book a yoga class at Yoga Energy.'

Kate's yoga studio, Yoga Energy, had just been incorporated as a company the week before. The logo had yet to be printed onto a physical business card. 'This woman called me at the hardest moment of my career. Moments before I had to submit the paperwork that would leave me financially vulnerable, and here was someone calling about doing a yoga class with me.'

After that phone call she said to herself: 'Yoga Energy has bigger plans for you now and you are going to be okay.' Resigning for Kate was still difficult and she was still in darkness, but the oppression had lifted just a little and, for a moment, some light seeped in.

You will experience moments of light during your dark night. Look for it.

We sometimes need to watch another's dark night to reinforce teachings from our own experience and to remind us that we survived – and not only survived but eventually thrived. I was reminded of my own increased strength and wisdom, a positive side effect of the Courageous Path.

In the weeks that followed there were long calls and text messages with Kate reassuring her she would be able to pay her bills, the yoga studio would succeed and she was making the right decision. The dark night does not call for a rational response; just reassurance so you can lean into its forward pull and it can take you where you need to go next.

I knew Kate's dark night was an essential part of her serving her community, not only as a yoga instructor but as someone who could transform her own life and continue to transform. To stand and lead yoga classes in her community she needed to know her own courage, her own strength, and to be reminded of her conviction to do this. The irony was that Kate probably thought she was courageous every day in the police force – and she was – but the most courage she had shown in her life was leaving her old life behind and being brave enough to follow what the universe was calling her to do, with no certainty that it would work out.

Kate had to become courageous first to lead others. The dark night was her initiation.

WHEN THE DARK NIGHT MAKES SENSE

You have a substance to your life if you've felt pain. You've got understanding, that's where compassion is. It makes you a deeper, richer human being.
LEIGH SALES

The Greek word for 'crisis' means 'a turning point in a disease', or a point at which the disease can get better or worse. When we are courageous at the point of a crisis we stand to become the heroine of our life. An illness can take us to where our body is falling apart and then our life feels as though it is falling apart. It may be days, weeks, years or decades later that we realise our life is coming together and that there is a grand plan for us, but when it is dark it is hard to sit in the space where time feels eternal. The dark night of an illness will take you to the bottom of the ocean, where you will learn to hold your breath and potentially surrender to the pain, which was what happened to Dr Shauna Shapiro.

I met Shauna when she was leading a mindfulness workshop at Esalen, California. We were sitting in the outdoor hot springs staring up at the stars in the night sky. When we share stories from our lives, the stories, like stars, connect to form a constellation and the bigger picture of our life forms. In that moment we realise we have been preparing for our greater purpose from the moment we were born.

Shauna said: 'I had scoliosis from about the age of twelve years old. It had been fine, but I went every year to see the same orthopaedic surgeon. He would do this X-ray and tell me it looked fine. When I was seventeen I went in for a routine check up to tell him I got a scholarship to Duke University to play volleyball.

'I just remember him looking at me and saying: "Your spine has gotten so bad it is going to puncture your lungs. We need to operate." My whole life blew up, and I never played volleyball again. I was in a hospital bed for six months. In just a moment my life changed.'

Sometimes the dark night will only make sense much later in life, and it can feel like a long time to wait. The reassurance is that it *will* make sense.

How often are we in the middle of an illness, a loss of a job or an ending of a relationship and it makes no sense? It is *meant* to not make sense. Trusting that it will eventually make sense is the only salvation.

Shauna continued: 'I landed in Thailand a year later. My girlfriend and I went to a monastery we heard was really special. We were not going there to meditate. Nothing was planned. When we got there a monk invited us in to meditate with him. My whole consciousness expanded. At the end of the meditation we sat with him for an hour. He looked at me and said: "Keep practising." A week or so later I went back and did a silent retreat, during which I had a profound experience of peace for the first time since my back surgery. I had been in pain every single day up until that point.'

Sometimes the dark night removes us from the pack. Shauna had missed her high school prom as she lay in her hospital bed, and she didn't go to the full moon party in Thailand as her friend did. She stayed with the monk and meditated.

I could relate to her experience of steering away from the norm. I left the pack of the corporate world and took a brief voluntary exile from my family and friends. In separating we are cut off from the familiar, but the solitude serves us as it is where we find the answers within. It is also where life can give us different answers from different people, or another point of view. It is a chance to press the reset button.

Years later Shauna was doing a master's thesis on the impact of mindfulness and meditation on medical students, on their anxiety, depression and empathy. An adviser said to her: 'You're going to ruin your academic career by researching meditation.' Many more experiences unravelled on her path, which helped Shauna get clear on her career intention, life purpose and calling. 'I actually didn't care about an academic career; I didn't care about making money. I really wanted to study mindfulness and I was like: "It doesn't matter if I ruin my academic career."'

As I watched Shauna's TEDx talk years later you would never have known of the curvature that was once in her spine. The dark night at the age of 17 took her on a long, meandering journey to finally standing in the spotlight on a stage in Washington Square and talking about mindfulness. Two million people have watched 'The Power of Mindfulness: What You Practice Grows Stronger' and have been shaped by Shauna's talk, but what they have really been shaped by is her Dark Night of Courage. She has the luminosity of a woman who has seen the dark, but she learned to see in the dark and now shows others how to do this.

The dark night may only make sense to you once you connect the dot in your life, which can only be done in hindsight. Do the challenging events in your life now constellate to reveal a bigger picture to you, one in which a greater meaning and grander plan is revealed?

Starting to make sense of the dark night moves you to insight and builds resilience.

TOOLS FOR YOUR DARK NIGHT

If all you can do is crawl, start crawling.

RUMI

The dark night does not call for a strategy or analysis: it calls for surrender, silence, intuition and trust; in other words, a spiritual approach. The teacher within will then emerge. Our formal education system has let us down as we are not trained to be spiritual. The soul is constantly trying to teach us, especially when we pause.

Psychologists, coaches and mentors could not answer the questions that arose from my dark night. They held the torch, handed me the tissues and gave me sympathetic looks, but my soul wanted to be my teacher if only I would let it. The knowings came from my soul. I sat in the space of accepting the things I did not know. The spiritual wisdom I had been accumulating moved from theory and concepts found in books and social media videos into a personal regular practice.

During my dark night I began to ask myself different questions that no longer felt dangerous. The dark night experience will be shaped by the types of questions we ask ourselves and the effort we go to to answer them. There is a calling to heal emotionally, but first we must recognise how we are wounded and why.

The dark night is not a time for gratitude journals, as writing what we are grateful for can pull us away from the melancholy that is trying to teach us to reach for something new. Gratitude journalling at this time may also feel inauthentic, which will prevent us from accessing our own truths for the changes we need to make.

This is a time for 'awareness journalling', a time to ask questions to transform our thinking: to ask questions we were not prepared to answer previously because of the shame that may have been brought up or the terror of the action we need to take. We may also need to admit that we co-created this reality with the universe. After a combative dialogue with the universe I realised my internal mantra was speaking to the universe of the changed life I desired. The universe was actually giving me what I wanted, and from this conversation the gratitude came.

All along our soul might have been wanting the lessons, insights and learnings. 'In such a hard way?' we ask ourselves. 'No, but this is what you chose,' says the universe.

Awareness journalling will show us how to choose differently. It is your soul talking to you, and perhaps it is time to listen.

I had to learn to not pathologise my past and always make myself wrong. I was an expert at making myself wrong, so I sought out a counsellor to help me keep perspective, stay open and have faith. My spiritual faith waivered during my dark night; I recall thinking: 'If I am so guided by a higher power why am I being so let down by God?' My spiritual tools changed. I found that even my meditation practice ceased to work during my dark night as it was another act of doing, of reaching out for something when the answers were within. My meditation actually compounded the lethargy of depression, so mindful movement became a focus instead, with long walks and different routes that had no destination. The answers came to me as I walked in silent contemplation.

Tools for the dark night focus on catalysing you to think differently about a problem or pattern that has persisted in your life for a long time.

THE FINNISH ART OF COURAGE

Rather than the stamina to run up a mountain, sisu *is the strength it takes to put one foot in front of the other.*

JOANNA NYLUND

According to the World Happiness Report 2020, Finland was the happiest country in the world for the third year in a row. Why?

The Finns have something called *sisu*, which is a combination of bravado and bravery, of ferocity and tenacity and the ability to just keep fighting. More importantly, it is the Finns' favourite word! Culturally they are super proud of embodying *sisu* in the same way Australians are laid back, Americans are patriotic and Canadians are ice hockey mad. Finns actually use this word to describe their national character, and it is a massive compliment.

So are *sisu* and happiness linked? According to the Third World Congress on Positive Psychology in Los Angeles on 29 June 2013, 'sisu is described as a psychological key competence which enables extraordinary action to overcome a mentally or physically challenging situation . . . which enables the individual to tap into mental strength beyond their pre-conceived resources'.

Would this make you happy? Well, hell, yeah! The population of 5.5 million Finns are not only courageous, but they identify with this valour and place a high value on the quality within their culture. They continually expand their lives, working to overcome difficulties. This is fundamentally what is called a growth mindset in the Western world: what could be more brilliant than a whole nation embodying this?

In her book *Sisu: The Finnish Art of Courage*, Joanna Nylund wrote: 'We credit sisu with giving us freedom and perseverance. On the eve of a race or an exam, parents encourage their children to look inside themselves for sisu.' Just reflect on that for a second: with their children trained in the art of courage, can you imagine the kind of positive mindset they will have as adults? Can you imagine how much these kids would save on therapy as adults?

Expert Emilia Lahti, founder of the Positive Psychology Association of Finland, says: 'Sisu begins where our perceived strength ends.' When you enter the dark night you have definitely reached the end of your perceived strength and are about to embark on the unknown: the darkness we fear and struggle to be with. Just because Finnish winters are dark, long and snowy does not mean this is a nation that is depressed or even pretending to be happy. Not at all. Their resilience means they do not see the dark night as dark. They embrace the darkness and, if anything, with herculean strength face their internal emotional struggles head on. Would this make you happier? I would argue yes, that you can't stay in the dark too long with this type of thinking or a nation around you that values it.

I think what the Finns can teach us is that we must be able to critically handle the tough times when they hit (which they will) and discover individually how to be courageous in life.

NIGHT VISION

Challenges and responsibilities are an honour. They indicate that spiritually you are ready for greater things.
DIANA COOPER

Once we have been through a dark night we can all see in the dark. We develop night vision, perhaps a vision from the third eye. I can now see in the dark, although the silence during my first dark night was deafening. As I spent time awareness journal writing, going on long walks and enduring many hours of silent introspection, I needed to be deafened by the silence. I needed all my senses removed for a period of time so there was no choice but to seek the truth with my sixth sense. This tool was being sharpened.

To be courageous is to be able to see in the dark.

When we finally emerge out of the darkness we look at events in our life and at people differently. Our sixth sense, our intuition, has now been amplified. I realise I had to see the darkness within myself and my own life to access the invisible forces: my intuition.

When I enter a dark night now I feel better equipped: I have more courage that has been born from perspective and understanding about how the dark night serves our personal evolution on the Courageous Path. The pain, confusion and madness still exists – this is the process – but the surrender occurs much more quickly. I reach for lightness where I can and I have a big family of soul sisters who have survived their dark nights to support me. My soul mentors have lit the dark path for me when needed. The dark nights become a little less dark with some mastery and guidance.

Finally, the dark night will take you to a place where you can name your pain, describe its source and understand the impact it has had on your life. This is essential for moving forward on the Courageous Path.

COURAGEOUS TRUTHS

1. A dark night is a transformational experience and you will experience it as a crisis or a deep depression.
2. You might be tempted to resist your dark nights by keeping yourself busy; however, you are delaying the transformation that is needed.
3. Your life may need a pattern interrupt for the patterns in your life that are not working any more.
4. When your life feels like it is disintegrating it may, in fact, be being repaired and remodelled.

5. You will be permanently transformed after your dark night; this is the purpose it serves.
6. If you have been through your own dark night you are called to support your friends during their dark nights and to share your wisdom.
7. Your dark night may only make sense weeks, months and years later. Be patient and trust.
8. Awareness journalling is a necessary tool to assist you during your Dark Night of Courage.
9. You know your bravery when you survive your Dark Night of Courage.

GET CURIOUS QUESTIONS

1. Are you currently experiencing a Dark Night of Courage? How can you stop resisting it and surrender to the transformation offered?
2. What is your Dark Night of Courage teaching you about the changes you need to make in your life?
3. What can you let go of? What can you allow in?
4. Who is supporting you during your experience? Can you reach for support and receive love through this experience?
5. How can you find comfort in the solitude?
6. How can you patiently let time heal you?
7. Is a friend going through a Dark Night of Courage? How can you share your learning and experiences with them?
8. What have your dark nights of courage taught you about yourself?

POWER PHRASE

'My dark night is a transformational experience. It belongs to me, and I allow it to teach me.'

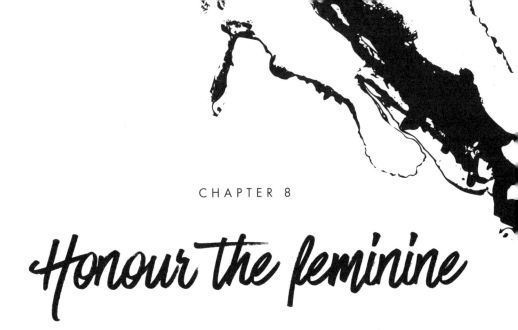

CHAPTER 8

Honour the feminine

Women do have a quest at this time in our culture.
It is the quest to fully embrace their feminine nature,
learning how to value themselves as women and
to heal the deep wound of the feminine. It is a
very important inner journey toward being a fully
integrated, balanced and whole human being.

– MAUREEN MURDOCK

The Courageous Path demands that we address and heal the neglected feminine aspects within ourselves; the world does not always honour the gifts of intuition and emotional expression. We have betrayed ourselves and the consequences have been great. Dependence on others for emotional support and approval leaves us with a depleted sense of self and no lasting commitment to our own authentic purpose. In order to reclaim the feminine within ourselves we need to understand how and why it has been supressed. This is a generational issue, and confronting the patterns experienced by the women who came before us may be the most profound, challenging and transformative work you do on your Courageous Path.

WOMEN HEALING THE MOTHER WOUND

If you want to understand any woman you must first ask about her mother and then listen carefully. Stories about food show a strong connection. Wistful silences demonstrate unfinished business. The more a daughter knows the details of her mother's life – without flinching or whining – the stronger the daughter.

ANITA DIAMANT

Our mother is our first love: there is no one else in our life with whom we have such a primordial relationship. For nine months in utero we are but one, beginning a process in the womb of inheriting an imprint from our mothers of what it means to be a woman. When a mother gives birth, a separation between the mother and daughter begins. Instinctively this can feel unnatural and requires great courage, but instinctively as a daughter grows it feels essential.

Bethany Webster, an expert in this subject, describes the mother wound as 'the pain of being a woman passed down through generations of women in patriarchal cultures. And it includes the dysfunctional coping mechanisms that are used to process that pain.'

I experienced so much conflict in wanting a career when my mother never had the opportunity to have one. When I visited my mother for dinner – late after work, dressed in my corporate suit and with no child on my hip – it felt as though my mother didn't see me, approve of me or love me. In her company I did not feel enough. Having aligned my path with the masculine, I was not comfortable with my choices in life so I created a safe distance between my mother and myself. These thoughts did not help me stand in my power in both the corporate world or in the family home. In *The Heroine's Journey,* Maureen Murdock dismantles this experience, explaining that our mothers were not given a chance to 'test their own skills and abilities in the male-defined world of remuneration'. In patriarchal societies our mothers were stripped of power and of the opportunity to follow their own paths.

What do we think happens to the emotional states of our mothers when they are forced to abandon their purpose, their childhood dreams? A rage builds. And when the rage is suppressed it transmutes into depression, neediness, shame and dis-ease. In these states our mothers emotionally abandon us because they have been abandoned themselves. There is a fracture in our emotional connection to the person we are most primally connected to that triggers instinctual fears within us in ways no other relationship will. In order to survive we abandon ourselves and our own emotional needs in the way our mothers did and enter a multi-generational cycle that is amplified and compounded with each generation. This is the impact of the 'mother wound'.

On the Courageous Path our tasks are to understand the dynamic that may have played out between ourselves and our mothers and to comprehend the impact and limitations this has created in both our lives. Perhaps we have been able to step onto and walk the Courageous Path, but we have not been able to fully reap the rewards or to stand in our complete power as we walk. Perhaps we may also self-sabotage, encountering problems with boundaries, giving our power away too easily, making ourselves small to be accepted, feeling unworthy and sacrificing too much as emotional caretakers of others.

This generational imprinting results in an unspoken dialogue between mother and daughter, who both want to be seen as all women want to be seen. Not honoured, revered, praised or applauded; just seen. When we are not seen we start to shrink, and when we start to shrink a resentment starts to build.

We need to examine the pain and unspoken dialogue that exists between ourselves and our mothers and in this way look at how we have contributed to this dynamic. I came to further understand the mother wound by listening to this unspoken dialogue, a dialogue that is not just about me but is about a shared experience of women across patriarchal societies:

Daughter: *Will you love me, Mother, if I am not the same as you? Will you love me if I walk in my own path – the path you could not choose?*

Mother: *Of course I will love you. But I don't know how to show you this love. I do not understand the life you lead. You say you are free but you don't appear to be happy, daughter. Your smile does not fool me. I am your mother; I know.*

Daughter: *You seem distant, Mother. You don't seem to understand my life at all. I am still sad inside. I am unsure why.*

Mother: *You are in a rage, dear child. When we talk I can feel your simmering anger. I don't know why you are angry at me all the time.*

Daughter: *You cannot show me the way in life. I must discover this on my own.*

Mother: *Can you not see me? Am I invisible to you?*

Daughter: *I must leave you now to find myself. I must go on this journey alone.*

Mother: *You are running away too fast. I cannot keep up.*

When we abandon the mother we abandon the daughter – ourselves. The Courageous Path involves questioning our relationship with our mother to start the healing process, although the questioning can feel loaded. If we dig deeper we are really asking: how did society let me down by limiting the mother's role and honouring the bravery and the purpose of the father?

To find our way back to ourselves we need to embark on a journey of self-mothering.

BEING MY FATHER'S DAUGHTER

Why is it that when women get passionate they're labelled 'emotional, crazy and irrational', but when men do they're seen as passionate and strong?

SERENA WILLIAMS

I am what is called a 'father's daughter', described by Maureen Murdock in *The Heroine's Journey* as 'a woman who has identified primarily with the father, often rejecting the mother, and who has sought the attention and approval from the father and the masculine values'.

My father was the second eldest of eight children – seven boys and one girl – so he knew how to raise boys. He wanted three boys and was blessed with three girls. My father's masculine nature formed a framework of values in our family, and I grew up being competitive with my younger sisters. I think I am innately competitive, but when the stakes are high for parental love so are the perceived rewards.

When you seek your father's approval you may seek to emulate him. I did, with the result that I made it to the end of one long road with a primary focus on my profession and I did not entirely like where I ended up. I wished I had walked a little differently, swayed my hips and slowed down instead of striding along with deliberate pace. I wished I had stopped to dance, to breathe, to listen. My hard-headedness was my north star guiding me. I spent such a long time during my life flexing and building up my rational and analytical muscles that my emotional muscles atrophied from a lack of use.

It isn't just tiring to always think and not feel; there is a brutality when you shut *her* down: your emotional side, your deep feminine side. It is self-abuse and self-denial.

When I did allow myself to feel I experienced a tsunami of emotions and ended up feeling as if I was not in control. My emotions did not envelop me in gentle waves so I could manage them or make sense of them. When things didn't go according to my plan I punished myself. During these times, no one held *her* when she needed to be held.

A patriarchy is a social system in which men hold the power and women are largely excluded. In a patriarchal world women cannot win. If we focus too heavily on caring and nurturing we are not visible, and when we are seen we are seen as being weak. We have little currency. If we choose the opposite direction of focusing on ourselves and our independent pursuits we are seen as being selfish. How do you choose when there is a steep price to be paid with either option? There really is no choice, is there? The impact of living within this patriarchal system results in constant inner conflict between being powerful and desperately seeking love. We are stuck between striving for success and anxiously attaching to love.

I turned myself inside out and upside down to walk, think and act like a man. In the corporate world this was rewarded with a princely sum: a ballooning salary, a title of importance and a secret club I could belong to. Some of the men on the ascent of my corporate ladder would shake my hand and pretend that I was invited to this club: the accountants' club, the bankers' club, the MBA club. Then I would make sure I was the best in the club, performing perfect cartwheels, a killer high kick and a distinction average at a minimum to ensure there would be no question as to whether or not I belonged. But the reality in this limited viewpoint was that I was a woman of colour in a male-dominated field of work. I didn't look as though I belonged with my tailored dresses, blow-waved hair and polished nails, and I never felt as though I belonged regardless of how much I tried. I never felt enough. My corporate life was a handmaid's tale.

Why was I trying so hard? Was there another club I needed to belong to? Then the real questions emerged: why did I need to belong to any club? Why was belonging to a club so important to me? Was there a different way to feel a sense of self-worth?

We must honour both our feminine and masculine natures.

MY UNHEALED HEART AND BODY

There is more wisdom in your body than in your deepest philosophy.

FRIEDRICH NIETZSCHE

My romantic relationships became a great testing ground for the mother wound. A strong independent woman, I would crumble into a needy, excessively insecure, co-dependent mess when I was in a relationship. I was anxiously attached when dating. I could not find a man who could love me when I was in my full power. I would stand, shoulders squared, demanding to be equal, yet how could they love me when I was yet to love myself in my full power? My relationships became the battle of the egos. Eventually, to ensure these men did not run away, I made myself less. I knew that I was copying an entrenched maternal pattern handed to me, but I did not know how to address it.

We all want to fall in love, yet no one likes to fall. We reach for a myth of romantic love and also run from the fear of the romantic subjugation handed to us by the mother's story. I was looking for a man to save me from the life I had created. When I fell in love I would anxiously attach to him, his friends, his spiritual beliefs, his routine and even to his favourite chocolate bar.

The author of *Women Who Love Too Much*, Robin Norwood, describes what I have experienced too frequently in my romantic relationships: that we will 'feel at home with people with whom our earlier unhealthy patterns of relating are recreated, and perhaps awkward and ill at ease with gentler, kinder, or otherwise healthier individuals'. This leaves us with a longing that can never be fulfilled and a sense of despair we turn in on ourselves. This was a permanent feature in my romantic relationships: working so hard to earn love and yet constantly questioning if I was worthy of love. During these times my inner mantra was:

Am I enough? Will you love me? Please don't leave me.

These are not courageous words. These are not the words of a woman committed to listening to the voice of her soul and following her calling. These are the words of a woman who walked and danced with fear daily. And when I came up for air to look at my purpose I was mentally and emotionally exhausted. Resisting loving ourselves is draining, as an inordinate amount of attention and focus is placed on the relationship. Holding on to my romantic relationships became my purpose, which they clearly weren't.

On the Courageous Path we must learn to stay loyal to our own ambitions, our dreams, our purpose. Our mothers may not have been able to teach us this. The Courageous Paths of women ask us to go beyond our mothers and for our daughters to go beyond us.

I didn't realise how much I needed to heal the mother wound until an orange-sized fibroid growth had to be removed from my uterus. Thoughts are powerful forces and can create dis-ease in the body; my angry, sad and depressed thoughts were a symptom of an unwell mindset that created a sick womb. Because I did not do the work to address my thought processes, after the major operation on my uterus the fibroid growth grew back even larger within two years. I had been stalling the inner work. According to Louise Hay's book *You Can Heal Your Life*, my heavy menstrual bleeding was asking me to question where was I leaking energy from: 'Nursing a hurt from a partner? A blow to the feminine ego?' I reflected there had been too many heartbreaks.

I have spent my entire life trying to be seen and trying to be significant. I was scared to become invisible, so my body manifested an illness to prevent this from happening. A healing needed to take place.

Your womb is telling you how well you honour your feminine nature.

THE JOURNEY OF HEALING

The mother wound is bigger than each of us.

DR CHRISTIANE NORTHRUP MD

Bethany Webster said: 'Healing the mother wound is not about hating our moms; it's about saying "No more!" to the patterns of shrinking, competition, unworthiness, self-hatred, and every single limiting belief system we want to shed because it's simply not ours but has been handed to us generationally.'

A step on your Courageous Path to heal the mother wound is to ask what your mother's relationship was like with her own mother and what was her experience of the mother wound. Sometimes you need to look back before you can walk forward.

Responsibility for ourselves is a key factor in healing the divide between ourselves and our mothers. We must ask ourselves: 'What part have I had to play in this relationship? What can I take responsibility for?' It was a challenging moment when I realised I had to take complete responsibility for the relationship I had created between my mother and myself, but when I took responsibility a shift happened that saw the dissolving of my judgement of my mother and how I wanted her to show up in my life. I realised that stepping into my power did not have to mean stepping away from my mother, but I did need to shed the social stereotypes of the woman I thought I needed to be: silent, sacrificial and obedient.

I have a mother who has exceptional intuitive abilities, a pious heart, a great sense of humour, a generous spirit and a mane of curly hair, all things she gifted me that I now embrace as a part of who I am and which were essential for my own Courageous Path.

Understanding the relationship our mothers have had with their own mothers will open a doorway to healing.

BEING SEEN

We are so busy teaching girls to be likeable that we often forget to teach them, as we do boys, that they should be respected.

SORAYA CHEMALY

All mothers are shamans. Rebekah Fisher, a good friend who is a birth doula, says: 'Giving birth is one of the oldest shamanic practices.' Shamans facilitate healing for individuals, groups and the community. In tribal cultures they often experienced an illness that gave them the insight they needed to heal themselves, then they shared those insights and brought their wisdom to their people. This is the journey of a woman; this is the journey we must take on our Courageous Path. When not medicated and ignored our monthly menses can be a deeply shamanic time during which our intuition is heightened and our feelings sensitised. Every month we stand to emerge healed and wiser from the experience should we allow it.

After our mothers birthed us they, and we, became conditioned by a world they did not create. On the Courageous Path our job is to rebirth ourselves into a new life created by design and not by pre-existing antiquated rules.

During my pilgrimage to the Amazon I was sitting at the feet of a female shaman in an ayahuasca ceremony in Peru and the medicine I had drunk had just started to take effect. I was sitting in pitch-black darkness when a deep voice spoke to me in my ear: 'You are here to release the rage of your mother's ancestors. We will be gentle with you.' I intuitively knew what this meant but panicked and resisted the waves of emotional pain.

When we resist life becomes harder, so I stopped resisting and allowed the flood gates to open. For five hours I silently screamed and openly sobbed; crying is a purge. I cried unwept tears for my great grandmothers, grandmothers, mother, myself and the children not yet born. I was releasing the trauma that had been handed down from generation to generation like precious outdated crockery. I could feel the presence of my ancestors supporting me through this physical and emotional process. At the end of the journey there were no more tears to cry; I inhaled deeply and howled at the full moon. I was no more a domesticated dog – caged, trained, obedient and compliant – instead becoming a wolf, wild and free.

Clarity came as I howled: my resentment against the feminine beliefs in society were holding me back. Even though my mother saw me I still felt unseen, and that gave me an excuse in life to act out, to not be responsible, to be angry, to be a victim. She had been my scapegoat for all I lacked. The worst thing I realised was that my mother had never been seen by her own daughter; she had been rejected by me. I needed to stop and witness her gifts as strengths, not weaknesses. When I did this I was able to witness my own gifts and a process of self-mothering began.

I did not need to save my mother; I needed to see my mother.
When I saw my mother I saw myself.

When I stopped rejecting who I was in the world I could finally stand in my power and call myself a professional medium. I could say the words out loud without wincing and expecting a negative response. I had to fully embrace my feminine nature and intuitive gifts, and heal the deep wound of the feminine.

When we were children my mother talked about dreams, past lives, premonitions and visions that came to her. She would describe the voices that spoke to her. I found this part of my mother mysterious and would sit back and ask questions. When I shut this ability down as I grew up, she did too. The umbilical cord of self-judgement joined us. On my Courageous Path, when I accepted, harnessed and used my intuitive abilities I noticed that my mother did also. I started to feel differently about my mother and our relationship: we were seeing each other for the first time through new eyes, through a lens of respect, reverence and acknowledgement. Our gifts became visible to ourselves and each other.

Chronic self-sacrifice over long periods of time – well, that is trauma that is against the natural state of a woman. Trauma can leave a chemical mark on a person's genes that is passed down to subsequent generations. Epigenetic gene expression means that the feelings, traumas and memories of previous generations may be experienced as truth even though the environment is different. The core belief of the mother is 'there's something wrong with me'. When I asked myself 'Am I worthy?', I realised this was not my voice but was a voice from many generations ago.

Being *seen* in the world is how we heal. We do not only need to walk the Courageous Path for ourselves; we need to walk this path for our children and humanity.

MOTHER WISDOM

When a woman tells the truth, she creates the possibility for more truth around her.
ADRIENNE RICH

The more stories we have of the courageous woman, the divine feminine and the heroine, the more memories we stand to build for the collective. In *The Awakened Woman* Dr Tererai Trent states: 'The world needs a cadre of awakened women – women in touch with the divine in them, women empowered by their femininity, women cultivating their sacred dreams and by doing so nurturing purpose in all women.' As all women walk on the Courageous Path, acknowledging and embodying the divine and healed feminine, we are giving birth to a new world.

Stepping into our power involves reclaiming our voice, which on the Courageous Path involves speaking about our own Courageous Leaps. It is important to ask our mothers questions about their lives and their mother's lives, inviting our mothers to share their dreams and ambitions.

We speak of the virtues and wisdom our mothers hold. Mother wisdom is acknowledging the gifts that have been handed to us genetically down the maternal line. Mother wisdom is the opposite of mother wounding: it involves seeing beyond the wounding. We all have wounds, yet we are not our wounds.

I have come from a line of strong woman, strong because they had to endure difficulties. My mother had an arranged marriage and migrated to a new country, leaving behind her whole family at a young age. My grandmother's husband died suddenly of a heart attack when she was in her 40s. Strength, tenacity and resilience were generational virtues handed down to me.

When we disconnect from the patriarchy of yesterday we stand to recreate a healthy relationship with the feminine and the masculine. As one woman rises so do we all rise. Remember that we need soul tribes to find where we belong, to be witnessed and to assist us to find synergies in our purpose. Dr Tererai Trent said: 'When we collectively tell our stories, we reveal the richness in that diversity and we create a beautiful cross-pollination of lessons to teach and strengthen each other. Sharing the mother wounds and mother virtues, helps all the mothers and daughters to heal. We are indebted to each other to do this for one another.'

All of us have mother wounds to some extent; generational differences and discord with the patriarchy through generations means no one really escapes this fate. What varies is how significantly the impact presents itself in your life: it may be a shadow you need to walk with, or the wound may run deeper and require deeper healing to transform your life.

I see you, Mother. I honour you for the Courageous Path you have walked.
I see you, Daughter. I honour you for the Courageous Path you have walked.

My mother is the kind of cook I know I will never be; time, patience and a love for cooking are something I haven't yet cultivated. I was eating my mother's famous chicken curry, and with each delicious mouthful I was in reverence of her craft.

She described how my grandmother used to cook and how cooking techniques have changed. My mother had premade a small bag of spices for me to take home: a time saver, she explained as she knows I have a busy life.

The topic suddenly changed to how I was named: my father named me. Our name is the unique word we hear the most in our individual lives. We are called to embody our name or to learn the lessons offered by our name. In Australia, 'sheila' is a word commonly spoken by Australian men to refer to a girl or woman and can have a derogatory connotation. As a part of reclaiming the feminine on my Courageous Path I had to overcome what 'sheila' meant to a man and redefine what 'sheila' meant to a woman – and, most importantly, what it means to me.

On the Courageous Path, when we heal our feminine wounding we stand to create a new world for ourselves. Each step we take through the healing process is a step closer towards reclaiming our power, stepping into our authentic self and ultimately into the courageous life we are seeking.

COURAGEOUS TRUTHS

1. You might be seeking approval and acceptance in a world that values women behaving in a particular way. This is changing. You can individually be the change.
2. Your task is to understand the unhealthy dynamics that may have played out between yourself and your mother. This was handed to you. Healing this is an essential step on the Courageous Path.
3. You don't have to turn yourself inside out or upside down to walk, think and act like a man.
4. Your body, womb and romantic relationships will tell you how connected you are to your feminine nature.
5. See the women in your life; witness them for who they are. All women, including you, want to be *seen*.
6. The healing of the mother wound will be the most challenging and transformative work you do on your Courageous Path.
7. The power of telling women's stories, including in your family, will heal in profound ways. Listen to the stories, write the stories and share the stories.

GET CURIOUS QUESTIONS

1. What is your relationship like with your mother? What is her relationship with her mother like?
2. What do you know about your mother's childhood and adolescence?
3. How do you sacrifice yourself in romantic relationships to hold on to love?
4. Do you lose your commitment to your purpose when in romantic relationships?
5. What is your womb trying to tell you? Are your periods heavy and painful?
6. How can you let yourself be more fully seen in your life?
7. What gifts are you most grateful to your mother for?

POWER PHRASE

'I honour my feminine self and all parts of myself.'

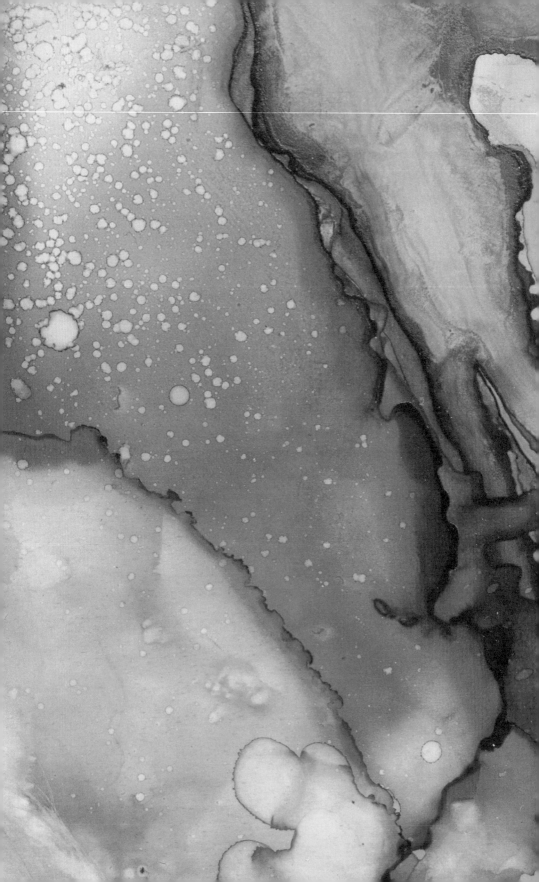

CHAPTER 9

Trust the universe

> A certain amount of desperation is usually necessary before we're ready for God. When it came to spiritual surrender, I didn't get serious, not really, until I was down on my knees completely.
>
> **– MARIANNE WILLIAMSON**

HAVE FAITH IN THE UNIVERSE

There is a lot that is demanded of you on the Courageous Path: resilience, persistence and strength. A meaningful life does not mean an easier life, but your yearning for meaning will draw you along the path no matter how difficult it is to follow. At times you will not have all the resources needed to continue, but trust that the universe will support you and help you in ways you cannot help yourself. There are many words to describe the unlimited consciousness of the universe: God, Source, Spirit, Higher Power, Jesus, Krishna, Buddha, The Great Mystery; it doesn't matter what term you use.

I was in a circle at a Narcotics Anonymous (NA) convention holding two strangers' hands. The voices of over 200 people – clean, sober and on the straight-as-an-arrow path – said in perfect unison the Serenity Prayer.

God, grant me the serenity to accept the things I cannot change, the courage to change the things I can, and the wisdom to know the difference.

I could feel this mantra vibrate through the floorboards under my feet. My partner had been clean from an addiction for four years and I was at the NA convention to support him.

In 1953 the universe spoke to Bill Wilson, the co-founder of Alcoholics Anonymous (AA). His biography *Pass It On* documents how Wilson was known for engaging in psychic and mediumistic pursuits. The universe spoke to him, and what he wrote down became the 12-step program for healing from addiction. This program is for the brave and courageous. Wilson wrote in step two: 'Come to believe that a power greater than ourselves could restore us to sanity.' The Serenity Prayer recited at the opening of an NA or AA meeting is about surrender.

But what or who are we surrendering to? According to Bill Wilson, we are surrendering to the universe.

You may have been conditioned to believe and possibly fear God or that God, unicorns and Santa all hang out in a distant imaginary land. You can lose your connection to a name. Just know that a connection to a powerful energy beyond you is an essential element you need to be courageous. During your Courageous Leaps, dark nights of courage and the space in between you need to know that someone or something is looking out for you: the same someone who called you forward to start walking the Courageous Path. If you don't believe that the universe is guiding you it is easy to believe you have been forgotten.

The Courageous Path involves initiations; this is where the fabric of your character is built. During this time you will definitely wonder if the universe has your back. The initiation at this point on the path is asking you to reach further into trusting the universe. When a child learns to walk their mother stands with arms outstretched and the child reaches their own arms out. The momentum of their body leaning forward, together with trust, allows the child to take their first few steps. The mother could step forward but she doesn't, as she knows this is how a child learns to walk.

This is one of the first initiations we all pass: the universe, like our mother, has our back. We must step forward on the Courageous Path knowing that the universe will catch us if we fall. This is faith.

The universe has your back. It takes courage to believe this.

My mother is a devout Hindu and prays every day. When we stopped playing as children and needed to find our mother, if we couldn't see her around the house we knew to look in the prayer room. While growing up I resisted Hinduism or any religion, so it is ironic that I have come to walk such a spiritual path. I was the most unlikely of her three children to do so, as I was rebellious and a contrarian when I was younger. The Courageous Path asks us to find faith, not necessarily in religion but in the unlimited consciousness of the universe. My mother showed me the power of faith.

To make courageous choices in life it is essential to know there is a powerful force guiding you. Even more importantly, it is essential that you connect and engage in a regular dialogue with this force.

DIALOGUE WITH THE UNIVERSE

Prayer is when you talk to God. Meditation is when God talks to you.
YOGI BHAJAN

When we start a new habit we are giving ourselves a chance at success. In *The Power of Habit*, Charles Duhigg said: 'Habits are powerful, but delicate. They can emerge outside our consciousness, or can be deliberately designed . . . They shape our lives far more than we realize.'

Journal writing is a powerful habit to start doing daily as a morning practice. If you told me when I started out on the path that I would have filled 21 journals from cover to cover over the course of five years, I would not have believed you. I didn't have time for journal writing in the early days, and I didn't realise I could choose to make the time. I just didn't understand how writing your thoughts and feelings down could help solve life's problems.

My psychologist couldn't be there handing me Kleenex tissues in the morning after my break-ups and bad dates. My best friend could not be there as I was crying myself to sleep when I was struggling to find a job, still unemployed and with bills mounting. I had to find another support structure. After another bad break-up I found myself lying like a starfish on my living room floor next to an empty box of Lindt mint chocolates. Teetering on the edge of a diabetic coma, I knew I had to stop repeating the same old relationship patterns.

As with turmeric lattes, macramé and mandala colouring books, I decided to give journal writing a go. Was it a fad? I didn't know, but the next day I started. I tried a new habit as at that stage I was willing to try anything. Emotional pain can be a powerful motivator for change. At first I wondered who I was writing to: Myself? God? The universe? And what was I writing about? What was I asking for? Was I doing this right?

I didn't realise it at the time but I was having a dialogue with the universe. I didn't acknowledge the universe for a long time. Ironically, I had a need to control everything yet constantly felt powerless. Those are the feelings of being disconnected from the universe.

When I started journal writing I started writing about my fears: I needed to see the fears in writing, to look at them and question: are these fears true? Are they real? Then I started writing about my hopes and dreams, which began a process of manifesting. As I wrote about my hopes and dreams I could see myself daydreaming about possibilities, then feelings about that newly created life would arise. More importantly, I started writing about what I was grateful for. The looping of my negative thoughts reduced, and I became aware of my thoughts via journalling.

The act of journal writing helps to arrest the negative thoughts that are not serving us. Negative thinking blocks the presence of love in our life. The powerful teachings within Helen Schucman's *A Course in Miracles* guide us to simply gain a full awareness of love's presence in our own life. The text says: 'There are no idle thoughts. All thinking produces an experience, outcome or event. Our thoughts create our reality.'

The Courageous Path is a long and winding road and a regular dialogue with the universe is required. As I wrote daily I noticed the physical indicators of stress lessened: fidgety hands, my shaking right leg and my shallow breathing. They didn't disappear – that would take more healing and time – but it was a step in the right direction.

Journal writing is a written prayer; it is a written meditation. It is a mirror for what is in your mind, and the habit of journal writing facilitates your thoughts to become more positive and powerful. When journal writing, clarity and wisdom can unfold in your thinking, but first you must purge your unhealthy and unprocessed emotions.

The habit of journal writing strengthens our connection to the universe. The ultimate reward is that it strengthens our connection to ourselves.

LET THE UNIVERSE SURPRISE YOU

She was never quite ready. But she was brave. And the Universe listens to the brave.
REBECCA RAY

I have surrendered to the twists and turns in my life, thrown my hands in the air on the emotional roller-coaster ride and screamed my lungs out, letting life take me where it needed to. Not only have I felt the most alive, I have also felt the most aligned. The powerful force of trust has taken me to the exact right next destination.

Your life is not going to unravel at all in the ways you expect it to. Expectations are based on control and fear. As *A Course in Miracles* teaches: 'The presence of fear is a sure sign you are trusting in your own strength.' Can you surrender? There is a very good chance your life is going to turn out much better, but will you allow it? I assure you it will be different to the life you expected. The space between expectation and reality, where your life may not look right but feels right, requires trusting the universe. Will you trust in the strength of the universe and not your own strength?

Have you ever had a psychic reading where you didn't like what you were told? When I was in the throes of my corporate life a psychic told me I would work in a crystal shop doing mediumship and intuitive readings and that I would feel fulfilled doing this work. I have wrestled with my spiritual path the entire way, and I shook my head furiously at this new-age lady. 'There is no way I am working in a crystal shop!' I replied a little too loudly. I considered myself to be part of the new movement of intuitive healers: I was manicured and modern with no dangling multicoloured earrings, head scarfs, kaftans or crystal ball gazing. I was judgemental and elitist and I still did not understand that the work I would be doing was one of service. I had also negotiated with the universe to do my calling part time.

Three years later I was on the cusp of burnout at my work desk. I had an overwhelming sense of hopelessness I could not shake. I was working as a medium for clients after work, but I was hungry to step wholly into this line of work and to serve more clients. I didn't know how to make the change.

The reality was that I feared change. I feared I would never have the strength to leave my corporate job. I feared if I did leave my job I would not make enough money to live on. I feared judgement from my family. Fear had shown up because I was not relying on the universe to help me. I had just come back from a spiritual pilgrimage to the Amazon and found an inner strength to make the changes in my life. When I tried to figure out the next logical step, fear stepped in and stopped me.

I exhaled deeply, pressed my hands together and rested them on my forehead. I didn't realise that I had put myself into a posture of prayer. I didn't realise I was about to speak to the universe. In desperation, I internally asked: 'Please help me to serve more clients. I don't know how to make this happen. Please help me.' I was taken out of this sacred silence by my phone ringing: it was another friend who was also a medium, working in a shop doing readings for clients.

'Sheila, you just popped into my head. I am not sure why. We are looking for another medium to work here on weekends. Would you be interested?'

My jaw dropped. Instantly, I said yes.

I just had a direct experience of speaking to and trusting the universe, and the universe delivered the answer almost immediately. When I stopped wanting things to be or look a certain way I was able to let in what was most in alignment in that moment. I allowed the universe to show me what was needed. Can our prayers be answered that quickly?

As the psychic had described, I started working in a crystal shop as a medium. The store was an esoteric wonderland filled with oracle decks, spiritual books and endless varieties of incense and crystals.

I had matured emotionally and my judgement had dramatically lessened. I wanted to heal and serve many more people, and it did not matter how that looked any more. When I walked into the crystal shop I felt as though I had arrived at some meaningful point on my Courageous Path. A few months into this new life and new work I smiled as I reflected on the psychic's words and my utter resistance to this new world that I could not then fathom or even understand.

We can never be sure what the universe has in store for us. Some of the small stepping stones lead to bigger stones, to ponds, to the river and then the ocean we are meant to swim in.

At the crystal shop I met my third significant mentor: she had the knowledge, wisdom and instructions for the next stage of my Courageous Path. This information had not been within my reach until I surrendered. We must walk through each door that opens for us without judgement.

Quite often when I undertake psychic mediumship sessions I see into a possible future reality that my clients cannot relate to or understand, and I acknowledge their resistance to a life that looks unrecognisable to them. I know I am helping them loosen their grip on their attachment to a life that looks a certain way and allowing the universe to surprise them.

When we allow the universe to surprise us we become aligned to the life we are meant to live.

SURRENDER TO MIRACLES VISION BOARD

First I dream my painting, and then I paint my dream.
VINCENT VAN GOGH

Many of you at some time in your life will have heard of the idea of a vision board. With vision boards we run the risk of only putting up pretty pictures of the objects, experiences and people we *know* we want in our life: a big house, a good-looking partner, laughter with friends, perfectly formed healthy children, an idyllic and secluded beach holiday. I have even Googled 'hot black brides' to find the perfect vision board picture of myself getting married (don't judge).

In life, big fat miracles *do* occur. I'm not saying don't do vision boards but be aware of how you do the vision board. You must create a vision board that assists you to manifest a dream you do not dare to dream and a vision that is unrelatable to you. What does this future look like? You need to create a vision board that makes space for the miracles in your life to show up while still holding on to the knowns, or the things you really do know you want in your life. Perhaps you need to create a *surrender to miracles* board.

How do we do this? We look to create feelings first, then perhaps the visions can assist us with the feelings even though the visions are not absolutes.

MELINDA: CREATING A VISION BOARD

That which you really, really want, you get — and that which you really, really do not want, you get.

ESTHER HICKS

Remember Melinda, who desperately wanted to become a mother?

'I come from advertising, so I am a visual person. My husband and I drew on an A4 piece of paper what we wanted in three to five years' time. You know, I'm rubbish at drawing. So we did stick figures. There was a picture of me with a pregnant belly. I'm holding hands with my husband, who has red hair. And then between us I drew a little boy and for some reason I coloured his hair a red colour. I don't know why I did that; I just did. And then behind us there was a house with a trampoline and there was an aeroplane going to see our family in the UK. I put it on a corkboard. That was the start of the vision board. It evolved from there. I would find magazines and cut out pictures that made me happy. There was a picture of a woman running into the water with her arms in the air, and if people gave me cards or if I found something cute I just kept on adding to this vision board. Really old school: paper on a corkboard. It grew organically over time. I didn't rush the process.

'In the process I imagined many extraordinary feelings: like community, connection, helping other people, feeling inner peace. The feelings just grew.

I did want a child, but when I look back I actually was putting up photos of a bigger life I wanted to live and I wasn't wedded to the photos. It was constantly the feelings that I focused on. It was such an emotional time.

'And it took five years for the boy to come to us. But you know what: I have a little boy with red hair.'

Melinda did the work on many personal areas to bring a child into her life. However, creating a manifestation tool was powerful and that was why she did it.

Vision boards rarely work on their own much like a piece of gym equipment that sits in our garage can't make us fit simply by existing. We need to engage with the board and feel into the board. We also need to surrender to the photos and pictures on the board and connect with the feeling. Why? Because it is so rare that life will turn out as we wish in the pictures. Most often it will turn out far better, but it may not turn out in the timing that we want: faster or slower, the universe will only meet us when we are ready. Holding on to the feeling on a daily basis is how we connect to the larger life we are creating.

I smiled, understanding that the wounded in us so often becomes the wounded healer. 'So with the creation of your vision board, it was like you were meant to be a mother but a mother and something else. You were in some way creating that bigger vision.'

'It is funny that you say that, because at my absolute lowest I met a woman who is one of the top fertility acupuncturists in Australia. We ended up having a conversation and I told her all the stuff I'd been through, which was a lot. I told her I also had studied to be a yogi. She said to me: "Gosh, if you can use this wisdom and knowledge later on that would be amazing." I was at the lowest point on my fertility journey, and it was the first time I thought: "Wow, you know, maybe this *is* something I could do later on."'

A seed had been planted in Melinda. Perhaps the seed had always been there, and this woman had fertilised the seed? Regardless, Melinda slowly started to create a vision of a greater life in which an important stage of her Courageous Path would be used to serve others. Melinda's larger life involved motherhood and running circles to support women on their courageous fertility path. Her yogi training and lived wisdom, triumphs and strength would be passed on to women in need of her teachings.

When we are creating our own miracle board it feels as though we are assuming we have power. Can we really create the life of our dreams? The truth is, we do have that much power.

COURAGEOUS TRUTHS

1. There will be points on the Courageous Path where you will be called to give up control of the outcome and surrender. Have faith in the universe.
2. Journal writing will assist you to have a dialogue with the universe.
3. When you allow the universe to surprise you, you become aligned to the life you are meant to live.
4. Create a vision board. Feel, believe and discover that you are a powerful manifestor.

GET CURIOUS QUESTIONS

1. Do you trust the universe? If not, how can you start?
2. Imagine what your life could look like if you had daily conversations with the universe.
3. Daily journal questions:

   • What are my intentions for the day?

   • What are my concerns for the day?

   • What can I give up worrying about today?

   • How can I show more love to myself today?

   • What am I grateful to the universe for today?

4. What feelings do you want to create in your life?

POWER PHRASE

'I trust in the universe to surprise me.'

CHAPTER 10

Spiritual toolkit

Intuition is the treasure of a woman's psyche. It is like a divining instrument and like a crystal through which one can see with uncanny interior vision. It is like a wise old woman who is with you always, who tells you exactly what the matter is, tells you exactly whether you need to go left or right.

– CLARISSA PINKOLA ESTÉS

Being courageous requires a spiritual toolkit that includes access to your intuition, regular contact with your spirit guides and a consistent meditation practice. You are about to start walking your path while being highly reliant on yourself for decision making. This is the way forward as you begin to realise you hold the tools for the journey on your Courageous Path. You have now started to trust in the universe, and when this waivers your spiritual toolkit will support you to bring you back into alignment with the support of the universe.

YOUR SIXTH SENSE

Cease trying to work everything out with your minds, it will get you nowhere. Live by your intuition and let your whole life be a revelation.

EILEEN CADDY

Intuition is the sharpest instrument in your toolkit. You must realise that your five senses are no longer enough and that being rational is not always what is needed. You are ready to reach into your sixth sense: your intuition.

Intuition is a superpower. It took me a long time to realise this, as I did not trust my intuition. There are two ways we learn about our intuition: by listening, and by not listening and paying a price. Both ways teach us. How often do we learn something from doing it the hard way?

The Courageous Path will open you up to your intuition. Your intuition has been speaking to you since the beginning of the Courageous Path, but you may not have realised this yet. Your intuition told you it was time to make a big change in your life, and when you ignored it you then experienced painful emotions, an ill body and mental inner conflict. The Courageous Leap you took was also guided by your intuition.

Noticing and acting on the signs you have been receiving was your intuition in action; you just never gave your intuition credit because you were desperate for change, so it didn't matter what catalysed the change. You must humbly let your intuition lead the way. Hearing, seeing and feeling your intuition is no longer enough. Acting and living your intuition is what is now called for, and it requires spiritual courage. Spiritual courage powers our intuition as an active force in our life, enabling us to listen to it, act on it and really trust it.

Understanding intuition has become a passion of mine. Now I use my intuition to help people through crises and major decisions. Before I stepped onto my Courageous Path I did not know when my soul was speaking to me and when it was just anxiety I had grown accustomed to living with. I had completely shut myself down. The thing with intuition is that it is such a powerful force, even when you shut it down it still gets through the cracks in your life to reach you. Your intuition never stops talking to you. Why? It is tuition from your soul, and your soul wants the best for you.

As a spiritual teacher I don't teach my students what intuition is. It is like teaching someone to breathe. I teach my students to have self-confidence and self-belief that the intuitive information they receive is the truth.

Caroline Myss, renowned author and speaker on spirituality and mysticism, states, 'Becoming a clear intuitive is the result of developing self-esteem. If you do not trust your inner self, you will not listen to your inner self.' To increase our intuition we must increase our self-worth. Why? We must believe we hold the truth and that it does not reside outside ourselves, that the truth does not lie with our parents, friends, boss or partner. The oracle that guides us lies within. Where there is doubt, fear or insecurities, intuition cannot reside.

Do you have the courage to become self-reliant? Can you live into your intuitive life and make decisions from this place?

At this point on the Courageous Path you cannot turn around. Why? When your intuition wakes you from the slumber of your unlived potential you cannot go back to sleep. You can never unknow that there is a purpose, mission, calling or greater meaning to your life. When you start using your intuition you cannot avoid connecting to your purpose and taking leaps and bold, brave actions.

Your intuition is your greatest power.
Trusting it turns it into your greatest superpower.

TURNING DOWN THE NOISE

Intuition doesn't tell you what you want to hear; it tells you what you need to hear.
SONIA CHOQUETTE

The gap between the rational advice or information we are given and what our intuition is telling us is called the *intuitive gap*. Analysing data in our lives is disorienting, as our lives are noisy: the cries of little loved ones, emails from our bosses and streams of visual messaging on social media. This noise creates a gap, and merely acknowledging the gap between rationality and intuition can be quite shocking. The rational information may come from safe and predictable sources: your friends tell you to stay but you know it is time to leave, or your boss promises something better around the corner but you know it is time to move on.

Confirmation bias causes us I have a theory, unproved and untested. My theory is that the closer we get to the depth of extreme emotional pain, the closer we are to our primal nature. This primal nature is the home of our intuition. To seek answers that keep us in our comfort zone, not answers we need to catalyse growth. Comparing and contrasting past and present experiences is exhausting and uses up a lot of energy. When we finally make a decision based on our rational mind we are still left second guessing. This is not what true intuition feels like.

When I realised I had to rely on my intuition I experienced a feeling of panic. Could I really rely on myself and not on others? Did I really hold the answers I needed? I had a feeling of loss, but was also buoyed by a reliance on myself. This was the healthy attachment I was yearning for, and was not reliance on everyone around me every time a crisis hit.

Intuition will provide you with information you have not previously had access to. The information will help you to understand your life purpose. The result being a quickening of your passage on the Courageous Path. You start to run on the path, but with freedom and in flow.

Intuition is most commonly received as a gut feeling, and intuition always has a physical intensity associated with the feeling. If it's the right choice you might feel as though a weight has been lifted or you may feel a force of certainty in your belly.

Knowing the difference between emotional anxiety and your intuition is a learned skill, as it takes time and effort to understand the subtle language of the heart and gut. Your intuition will become stronger the more it is honoured and valued.

What do you constantly feel in your gut?

INTUITIVE DOORWAY

I believe that your tragedies, your losses, your sorrows, your hurt happened for you, not to you. And I bless the thing that broke you down and cracked you open because the world needs you open.

REBECCA CAMPBELL

I have a theory, unproved and untested. My theory is that the closer we get to the depth of extreme emotional pain, the closer we are to our primal nature. This primal nature is the home of our intuition. In this primal state we become super sensitive and receptive, two key elements for accessing our intuition. Extreme emotional pain is accessed when we reach what I call the 'sacrificial limit point'. All women have this point, even the extreme martyrs among us. When we reach this point our intuition says: 'Enough is enough; you deserve more. What about you and what you want?' This is not self-love we are accessing; it is our instinct, it is our truth, it is our intuition.

The pain of deep heartbreak opened me to my intuition and cracked me open. After the heartbreak I was taught to walk through life with my heart wide open. Quite often our intuition opens after great heartbreak or grief from the death of a loved one. We access our intuition through our heart, which must be full and open. It requires courage.

When the relationship ended I would cry every day for weeks during my lunch break. I would sit in my car and sob. I would sip on coffee and cry till there were no more tears left. Not a single person knew of the hardships I was experiencing. I was unaware I needed counselling or simply someone to talk to.

Have you been in a position where you have become lost because you've given your heart completely to someone? Where do they end and you begin? This type of love is a choice and an action; it is irresponsible to your soul. There is a big, fat lesson waiting on the other side of the pain, but you must get through the pain in order to reach the wisdom.

How do we access our primal nature: through pain? Is this always the way? No, but it's common. Clients have come to me during a time of grief or crisis, then after they have gotten through the acute pain I see their transformation. Their intuition comes through strongly and the magic happens when they start to trust their intuition. It is pain that takes us beyond the perception of our five senses and to our sixth sense. Perhaps denying our intuition led us into the pain. Perhaps the lesson learned is to never deny our intuition.

A deeply painful experience in a woman's life is where she experiences the ultimate sacrifice of herself. This creates a doorway to accept and integrate her intuition. This is a point of no return.

THE NELSON MANDELA EFFECT

'Told you so.' Sincerely, your intuition.

ANONYMOUS

Intuition is a language of subtlety. It won't hit you over the head. The challenge with intuition is that it can come to you quickly – so quickly you just might miss it if you do not know to look for it. The voice speaking in your ear may only say something once, but are you brave enough to believe that voice? The feelings may come to you as one wave or repeatedly, but do you then self-medicate with coffee, sugar and social media to distract yourself from those feelings? The knowing may be there and may feel like it comes from the centre of your gut, yet you ask others for advice that you *want* to hear. The advice that keeps you stuck.

My finely tuned intuition meant that I touched Nelson Mandela, even though it was just a fleeting moment. I attended a British Red Cross humanity lecture in London at which Nelson Mandela had a conversation with a Red Cross volunteer who had visited him in prison. They had become great friends over a 20-year period. I was determined to be in the front row, so I arrived at the event two hours early and soon three more people joined the queue. Quick friendships were formed as we waited. When the doors were flung open there was a friendly rush to the front. We were crestfallen to see the first 10 rows had been reserved for dignitaries, politicians and journalists. Four of us were left dawdling, still unseated. How did this happen: we had been the first four in the queue!

Suddenly I heard a deep voice in my inner ear: 'He will be walking down the aisle.' My inner knowing was to trust the voice even though it didn't make sense to my logical mind. The front of the hall was lined shoulder to shoulder with heavily armed security, so I believed Nelson Mandela would be walking on and off the stage and not up the aisle. I turned to my newly made stranger/friends and said: 'He is going to walk up the aisle on the way out. Let's sit on the aisle further up the back.' They believed me and the four of us took aisle seats at the back. When intuitive feelings are spoken they have a resonance.

No one moved as Nelson Mandela spoke: we were all mesmerised by this man and his energy. You could hear the collective silent contemplation. We all inwardly thought: 'Could we ever have been brave enough to serve a life sentence to free a nation?'

The minute the last words left his lips we all jumped to our feet with a deafening applause. He stepped down off the stage to leave from the left entrance, the same way he had entered. Out of nowhere, he paused and looked across the audience, scanning the room. Perhaps Nelson Mandela was using his finely tuned intuition to know that he was safe and could walk with the people. He tapped a broadly built security man on his shoulder and pushed him to the side in a gentle way that only Nelson Mandela could. With minimal security, Nelson Mandela proceeded to walk down the aisle. I was jumping around and beaming like a mad woman.

When you know, you know. You must listen to the voice; you must quickly act on your intuitive knowing. I did. I touched Nelson Mandela's arm, and he looked squarely into my eyes. He didn't say anything, but I got to smile at him. It was a moment I will remember forever.

Sometimes your intuition will call for an immediate response; sometimes there is no time to think about it. From that moment I remember the sound of the voice and the certainty I felt when I heard it, and I locked that experience into my memory. Years later when I heard 'It is time to leave' I listened to the voice; thus I was able to repeat the process. The muscle used to listen to my intuition began to grow and flex.

The more we use our intuition the more we know the sound of that voice and the shape of that feeling. Can we listen and act quickly? Can we keep on doing this as a consistent practice on the Courageous Path?

MIND FULL OF STUFF

The purpose of training in mindfulness meditation isn't to become 'better' at meditation, but rather to become 'better' at life.
DR ELISE BIALYLEW

Your instrument of intuition will be sharpened by consistent meditation practice. Being courageous in life requires you to make decisions daily from a place of calm and clarity. It also means being prepared to stand in the storms of transition and manage your stress levels. You don't live a courageous life by standing still. You are striving to expand, and at times this can cause stress. Mastery of the Courageous Path includes learning how to manage your stress and anxiety, for which the greatest tool is meditation.

I have been my own lab rat testing this theory for 12 years. I know it's true because I have tried nearly every type of meditation style and have spent years meditating for 14 hours per week and then as little as 30 minutes a week. I have gone on silent retreats where there was nothing to do but meditate. I have also taken breaks from meditating when I needed to.

With so many variations in frequency and intensity, I now know that when I meditate I am calmer and life is smoother. My intuition is accessed easily and more accurately. The challenge I have found with meditation is that you don't know if it is actually working. When you start the discipline of going to the gym you can soon see that your skinny jeans fit again, and when you start art classes there is evidence that you can now draw. But how do you stick with a goal or a daily practice when you don't know that it makes a difference?

These days my approach to meditation is one where discipline meets compassion. There is an intention behind what I do but no mental reprimand when I don't make the time. It has taken me over a decade to realise this, and sometimes it just takes that long to understand something and cultivate a practice that works for you.

Let me fast track that process for you.

When I started my MBA many of my friends said I needed to meditate. I resisted their sage advice as I knew they didn't meditate so how could they know it would work for me? After a while I realised I could not cope with the mounting anxiety and stress of studying and working. I had spent years working on my physical body but had not put any emphasis on my mind. The mind can be a doorway to the deepest states of happiness or the deepest states of despair, so mastery of our mind includes mastery of our stress levels, which is essential for courageous living.

The changes in your life when you start mediating will be small. When you start meditating you will attempt to sit in stillness for a few minutes before rushing off to the demands of your hectic day. When you get up from your cushion you will exhale and tick that task off your to-do list. Sometimes you just need to trust science and the tons of compelling data that supports this ancient practice, that has stood the test of time. It is a practice that requires consistency and dedication when you begin.

The meditation myth is that the 60,000 to 70,000 daily thoughts you have will disappear when you meditate. When I lead meditation classes I usually speak about what we do if someone has forgotten to turn off their mobile phone during the meditation and it rings. I say that 'Life involves phones accidentally ringing; your meditation practice is no different. Life is imperfect and you will experience this in your practice. Be with the imperfection, be with the thoughts and always come back to your breath.'

The benefits of meditation are subtle, endless and permanent, as you are rewiring your brain. Mindfulness expert Dr Shauna Shapiro's life was changed by five words spoken to her by a monk in Thailand: 'What you practise grows stronger.' In her TEDx talk 'The Power of Mindfulness: What You Practice Grows Stronger' Shauna describes the cortical thickening and growth of new neurons in response to the repeated practice of meditation. 'Mindfulness works. It is good for you. It strengthens our immune functioning, it decreases stress, it decreases cortisol, you sleep better.' Dr Elise Bialylew, founder of *Mindful in May* and author of *The Happiness Plan*, states that: 'Ten minutes of mindfulness meditation a day over one month was enough to support more positive emotions, reduce stress, increase self-compassion and strengthen focus in daily life.'

You will need to experiment and find your flavour in meditation. There are many types to choose from: breath, loving kindness, chanting, body scan, visual guidance. You may find you want one practice in the morning and a different practice in the evening. Practice also means experimenting, as curiosity about meditation will allow you to explore and find the practice that works best for you.

Meditation gives you access to the part of yourself that knows the truth about the decisions you need to make in your life. Intuition is accessed when you are in a calm and centred state, and meditation is the doorway for this. Accessing your intuition and a calm inner state are essential on the Courageous Path.

Meditation supercharges your intuition.

YOUR BOARD OF SPIRIT GUIDES

Guides will help you achieve new levels of personal power and spiritual growth.

SANAYA ROMAN

Walking on the Courageous Path is a great undertaking. You may feel alone, but know that you never are. At some point your intuition will tell you it is time to meet the invisible team supporting you, your board of spiritual guides whose job is to make sure you fulfil your soul contract. What is your soul contract? That thing you have being searching for your whole life: your purpose, your calling, your dharma. Choosing to walk on the Courageous Path is fulfilling the contract, but sometimes you will want to stop, pause, turn back and go on detours. However, contracts are binding and feel binding, which is why you have a constant niggling feeling to move forward on the path. Your spiritual guides will help to keep you on track.

Activating your intuition is closely linked to meeting and knowing your spiritual guide team. How does this occur? You may be drawn to a workshop with a spiritual teacher who will help you. You may be drawn to a guided meditation, a visual visitation from your guides may occur in your dream state, or you may request that a spirit artist draw you a picture of them. Like an adopted child who may seek their biological parent at the age of 18, you too start the search when you reach maturity on the Courageous Path. You don't know where it will lead, but you won't stop looking until you have found your spirit guides. I know I didn't.

When I first heard the term 'spirit guide' many years ago two things happened. First, I had a massive 'aha' moment: I had felt there had been someone by my side for a lot of my life and finally that someone had a name or a form. Second, I was confused: I immediately wanted to give this spirit guide a race, age, sex and name because the analytical and logical me wanted to demystify the mystical.

It is spiritual law that you must request the help of your spirit guides to step forward. How do you do this? With a powerful prayer, meditation or just an out loud request to the universe, which I have done many times while alone in my apartment or out driving. I used to think it was super weird talking out loud, but I'm now comfortable with having these types of conversations. I think to myself:

'I am alone, so who cares what anyone thinks? I can do what I want.' Of course, you can have a silent internal dialogue with your spirit team.

Your board of spirit guides will change. Like mentors in life, you will require different types of support and thus different guides will step in to support you depending on what you need: personal healing, creativity, resilience, wisdom, reflection, ancestral healing or a higher level of courage.

In order for you to walk your Courageous Path you are going to need to listen, talk to and trust this team, which is always trying to telepathically send you thoughts, impressions, feelings and knowings. They are always trying to find the gap in your thoughts to do this, which is not easy and is why a still or active meditation is so important.

Commit to the practice of connecting with your spirit guides and you *will* encounter some profound experiences. There is a meditation at the end of this chapter to help you connect with your spirit guides.

Over the years of working with my own spirit team I have learned several spiritual truths I would love to share with you. I am not going to lie: it is going to take spiritual courage to believe. If you are a non-believer, that is okay, but just believe you are supported in some way by the universe. All I request is that you do not sit on the fence: use your spiritual courage to discover your own spiritual truths and how they can serve you.

Below are some spiritual truths I have collected on my path, and these are the principles I teach my students.

Master guide

The head of your spiritual team is your master guide, who has been with you since birth. Their job is to constantly connect you with your purpose in life and to ensure you learn your soul lessons and explore your gifts. When the chips are down the master guide will hold you closely and comfort you. You have already had some big and little experiences with your master guide; you just need to reflect and remember what they are. They were guiding you with signs early on your Courageous Path. Your master guide does not leave your side and can be called on at any time for guidance, wisdom and direction. I will show you how at the end of this chapter.

Gatekeeper guide

You have a gatekeeper guide who, much like the Unsullied commanders in *Game of Thrones*, offers serious bad-arse protection from harsher energies. Many students fearfully ask what the harsher energies are, and I always turn this question back to them: 'Who and what do you think are harsher energies? What have your experiences been? Your body and your mind don't lie to you.' Perhaps the harsher energies are people who don't make you feel good about yourself, who hold a constant negative mindset and are in victimhood. Perhaps they keep you stuck when you start talking about changing your life. Perhaps the harsher energies are more severe, and you experience bullying and great conflict with them. Hold them in a place of compassion, but also hold yourself in a place of greater compassion, with healthy boundaries. Use the gatekeeper guide to help you navigate your relationships with any harsher energies you experience as you ascend on your Courageous Path.

Ancestor guides

Ancestor guides assist in the healing of family patterns that reveal abuse, sublimination, not speaking up or claiming your truth or experiencing a lack of self-worth. You are seeking to make sense of these patterns as they are door stops to stepping into courage and authenticity.

Many years ago I would sit with a medium and converse with my grandmother. I did not know my grandmother well when she was alive as she lived in Malaysia and I lived in Australia, but after she passed away we got super close. Any time I saw a medium she was the first one to come through to speak to me. Once when I was in my 20s I was so angry with my father that I said to the medium: 'Ask my grandmother why my dad is the way he is? She was his mother; she should know.' The medium's eyes opened wide: I think she was surprised at my frankness. She replied: 'You must have patience with your father, as this is how he is and always has been. Have compassion.' I felt the tension release from my body: it was as though my grandmother was the only person who could have told me this.

Ancestors are always working with you to keep the family healing, to help you realise what patterns you are perpetuating and to lift your awareness so you can break cycles that may be repeating. They assist with strengthening and shifting family dynamics so that internal harmony and peace can be worked towards.

BE STILL PRACTICE: CONNECTING WITH YOUR SPIRIT GUIDES

When wishing to connect to your board of spirit guides you can request that their energy step forward to reveal themselves to you. Each spirit guide will be serving you in various ways and will feel different as their energy connects with you. You can explore connecting with them by invoking their energy with the following practice:

- Find a comfortable sitting position, then close your eyes and centre yourself.

- Clear your mind, letting go of any tension and stress for 30 seconds. Breathe in and out within a space of stillness, allowing your exhale to be longer than your inhale.

- Visualise yourself in your own bubble of pure white light. Set an intention internally that the bubble of divine light is charging, shielding and protecting the outer layers of your energy field.

- Request in your own silent inner voice: 'I call upon my spirit guide team to step forward into my energy field to make a strong and clear connection with me.' Feel their light building around you in a circle of light.

- When you are ready, say: 'One guide please step completely into my bubble of white light now.'

- Try to become aware of any changes taking place around or in your body. Perhaps you will feel the vibration around your body quickening or feel a sensation of heat or cold around your body.

- Progressively set up a dialogue with your guide by asking them questions and being present with where your mind goes, because the information they send you will be relevant to the images or the timeframe they have come from. Call in your strongest guide to step forward.

- Asking open questions is most helpful, including: 'Show me what I need to know now', 'Show me how to heal' or 'What are my next steps?'

- Thank them for connecting with you. Next, ask them to step back and out of your energy, allowing about one minute for your guide to fully step out of your field. Thank them for their presence.

- Thank and release the circle of guides supporting and holding your energy within the bubble of light. Start to feel yourself gently separating from the higher vibration of your spirit guides, again allowing them a minute to release from your energy field.

- Start to bring yourself into the present moment by breathing deeply, becoming more focused on the here and now.

- Open your eyes.

Write down each experience, journalling what you can remember from each time you connect with your spirit guides to gain a greater understanding of the relationship you have with them and why they support you. Each time you deep dive to connect with your guides, do not worry about the information you are getting; just let it flow in and have no attachment to what you receive. Allow the experience to go where the intention to connect to their energy wants to go.

Please note: once you allow a spirit guide's energy into your energy field do not break off to make notes, as it will be hard to make a connection with them again. Sit in the energy and ask questions, and write up the wisdom after the experience. Don't worry if you forget parts of it, as that is normal with the process of connecting when you are first starting out. The wisdom can be accessed again.

COURAGEOUS TRUTHS

1. Trusting your intuition guides you on your Courageous Path. At some stages on the path your intuition will be the only tool to direct you forward.
2. Trusting your intuition requires spiritual courage and great self-belief.
3. Painful experiences in your life can open you up to your intuition.
4. A noisy life will block your intuition.
5. You will be required to make courageous transitions and take bold actions on your path. This forward momentum can create stress and anxiety. Meditation and mindfulness are necessary spiritual tools to give you access to a state of calm.

6. The primary role of your spirit guides is to ensure you are living your life in alignment with your purpose.

7. Creating a daily or weekly practice will develop a relationship with your spirit guides.

GET CURIOUS QUESTIONS

1. Describe a time when you trusted your intuition. How did it feel?
2. Where is mindfulness already working in your life?
3. What nourishes your mind, body and spirit? Can you give yourself this gift every day?
4. Describe your spirit guides. What are your spirit guides telling you?

POWER PHRASE

'My intuition always honours me.'

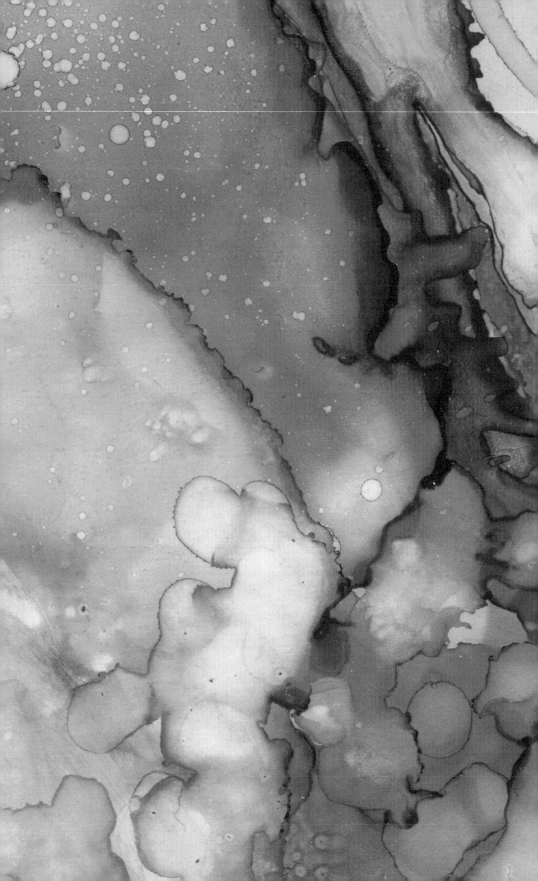

CHAPTER 11

Courage to be you

Every individual matters. Every individual has a
role to play. Every individual makes a difference.

– JANE GOODALL

You are ready to authentically live a life of no regrets, that is pregnant with possibilities. It is at this point on the Courageous Path that you realise that you are walking on your own path. You are ready to harness your unique gifts, your wisdom and your knowledge to make sense of your life experiences: the tragedies and triumphs. This is the part of the path where you rise and are seen. You are ready to share *you* with the world.

RUBY: OUR UNIQUE PURPOSE

It might have been done before, but it hasn't been done by you!

– ELIZABETH GILBERT

Are you unable to see how special you are? How common is this?

Our unique awesomeness sits in our own blind spot. Whether it is the stuff in our childhood that shaped us, or the knowledge acquired over years of observation or significant events that stand out, it always appears to be so ordinary to ourselves while being extraordinary to the onlooker. And here's the deal: it is in our knowledge, life experiences and accumulated wisdom that our gifts can be found. We are called now to make sense of and use these gifts for something bigger than ourselves. Do we all have a purpose that is bigger than ourselves and that involves service? Yes, we do.

Ruby Lohman is the stepdaughter of a funeral director: the first car she drove was a hearse, her stepfather would regularly bring leftover flowers from funerals home, and talking about death over the dinner table was commonplace.

Years later Ruby is sitting with 20 strangers at a long table covered with delicious food and wine. There is anticipation, even though no one knows what to expect, and you can smell the subject of death. It is a death dinner party, a concept co-founded by Ruby. The premise is simply 'We get together, eat great food, drink great wine and talk about death.'

Up to 50 people attend these events, which feature speakers such as grief counsellors, grave diggers, end-of-life consultants and palliative care nurses. She even had a speaker who had clinically died for several minutes who shared his near-death experience.

'The response from the attendees has been overwhelming. Everyone has been waiting to have these conversations and here's the space where they can do it.'

It was obvious to me that Ruby's background had played an important part here: 'Ruby, do you feel this is your special thing to offer the world?'

'What, who me? Gosh, I don't know.'

After her initial reply, Ruby reflected on my question. She was not aware of how unique she was, as her childhood had seemed so ordinary.

'Some days my stepdad would pick us up from school in a hearse. You know, death was a very day-to-day thing for me growing up. I guess because of my childhood, having some knowledge about death takes you a long way towards feeling more comfortable about it. I found it strange as an adult that so few people talked about death. I think I needed to have a level of comfort with death to start something like the death dinner parties.'

On the Courageous Path one of the biggest obstacles of stepping into your larger life and purpose is thinking that you have nothing unique to add, that it has all been done before. You overlook your own specialness. Watch the reactions during conversations you have when you talk about your life, which will provide feedback about why you are special if you can't see it yourself.

Ruby said: 'It really is the one thing we one hundred per cent all have in common as humans: death.'

I laughed. 'I think there are two things we all have in common: death and our own unique purpose.'

The death dinner party concept is not original. Is it very common for people to sit around talking about death? No, but there are a load of people around the world who have been just as fascinated as Ruby, have had a connection with death and created a similar type of event or experience for their community.

Ruby said: 'My friend's dad had been diagnosed with cancer. It was the first time she had really been confronted with death. My friend wanted to talk to someone but felt there was nowhere to go to. I'd heard about these events in the USA where people got together over dinner and talked about death, and I just thought that sounded like my dream night out.

'I remember going home and feeling so alive with this idea and waking up at five a.m. the next morning. I was brimming with inspiration.'

Those are the feelings you have when you are smack dab in the centre of your purpose: inspiration, fulfilment and generosity.

'It really was simple: there's this huge thing that affects all of us, but there's nowhere to go to talk about it. So my friend and I got together and thought: why don't we make it happen?'

Ruby and her friend did not let themselves get overwhelmed by thinking too big: they just wanted to serve, so they started with their local community. They put their hands up to the universe and said: 'Yep, we are qualified for this, we accept the job.'

Your gifts do not have to be grandiose or make social media headlines, although they might one day. There is as much room for environmental activist Greta Thunberg to make a difference in the world as there is for you to plant a vegetable garden in your backyard that becomes a community garden or is an aspect of creative expression you share with your neighbours. Any contribution you make to those around you is of great value. This is the richness in life you are looking for.

The thing you are yearning to do probably has been done before in some way, but it has not been done by *you*, and you hold the special ingredient in your family, community, city, company or country. This is why the universe placed you exactly where you are.

Your job is to find out how unique you are.

YOUR GIFTS

There are far more people in need of your gifts than there are people giving those gifts.
GABRIELLE BERNSTEIN

I did not think talking to spirits was unique, as I grew up having a lot of esoteric conversations with my mother. As I shared my story with more and more people, what became obvious to me was a particular trifecta of uniqueness: being a finance director, a woman of colour at the corporate board table and a medium. My blind spot had been feeling accepted as a working medium, and it took others to point out to me that while there are a lot of mediums out there working, none were like me. I started working towards being a spiritual teacher for people awakening in the corporate world. In fact, I was able to have an impact on a lot of corporate people because I had an MBA, which meant I could easily bridge the business world and the spiritual world. I had the language and experience of both, which made me relatable.

My life started to make sense when I stopped and owned my unique life path. It was also then that I realised I had been training for my calling since birth. It is our job to reflect on our life and make sense of it as a training ground. If we don't do this it is an injustice to ourselves and those who need us most. Your gifts are born from time and pressure, much like a precious diamond. There are several important ways to mine your gifts.

Think about the unique abilities and skills you had growing up: perhaps you excelled at something as a child or were determined to overcome your limitations, or perhaps you showed tenacity that was perceived as stubbornness or sensitivity to others that was perceived as weakness. Either way, what was this?

Sometimes being born into what feels like a mismatched culture, family and generation is your biggest asset because you need to figure out how you do *you* when there is no external point of reference. I call this the Courageous X factor. I was an unmarried woman in a Sri Lankan culture where marriage is a priority. I now teach women how to honour their unique path purely because I had to honour my own. If I had settled down, got married early and had kids maybe there would have been no lesson. The Courageous X factor gave me the lessons I needed to learn.

Whether we feel misplaced or not, we all acquire knowledge from our environment. Perhaps what is normal for you is something others would love to know more about. You have learned a lot so don't take your knowledge for granted; this which is why self-awareness is so important. What do you know, drawn from your unique life experiences, that others don't and could benefit from? It is this unique knowledge that may help fast track and guide others on their own Courageous Paths.

How are you meant to fast track people? What gifts are you meant to share?

THE POWER OF SERVICE

Massive numbers of light-workers are focused on their own Spiritual growth and are not focused on the service work that they Spiritually contracted to do!
JOSHUA DAVID STONE

Your gifts are most probably born from high levels of empathy because the thing you needed to share with the world would have required you to face some sort of struggle, have discipline, make some sacrifices and persist. Empathy and your gifts are a powerful combination that will provide real service.

When people told me to share my unique gifts with the world I was overwhelmed. The world is a big place, and social media has made the world entirely accessible, borderless and sometimes incomprehensible. Where do you start? This type of thinking stopped me in my tracks, and I didn't do anything for a long time. Then I got inspired and took little steps. When I started out as a spiritual teacher and medium I thought small, really small, which was very different from my previous role in a global corporation where thinking big was commonplace. I offered my services to my local community and at local fairs, and I started a small meditation group in my home.

Think of the world as *your* world. The world is who you have direct contact with on a daily basis. You create your world and its borders. The only thing you are measuring when you share your gifts and talents with the world is how big your heart expands – and, trust me, your heart will feel enormous. Ruby gave the gift of herself to the world, bringing together her knowledge, wisdom and experience to serve a greater purpose. What did the world return to her? Her gifts were witnessed, and she was seen for who she was: a courageous woman.

We can't choose how or when we die, but we can powerfully choose how to live. We can be empowered to make sense of all the important markers in our life, the triumphs and tragedies, and to give the gift of ourselves to the world. Are you courageous enough to do that? Do you have the courage to see and appreciate that you *are* a gift?

ALL WOMEN ARE MEANT TO BIRTH AGAIN AND AGAIN

I think ageing is an extraordinary process whereby you become the person you always should have been.

CARL HONORÉ

In 1963 Japan began giving a silver sake cup, known as a *sakazuki,* to every citizen who reached the milestone of turning 100. In 2015 this tradition ended because Japanese centenarians were becoming too numerous and it was sending the Japanese government broke. Why was this happening? Because millions of Japanese have *ikigai*, which translates to the 'value for being alive': in other words, a reason to get up in the morning. In fact, the Japanese island of Okinawa, where *ikigai* has its origins, is home to the largest population of centenarians in the world. It sounds like there is a connection between living longer and *ikigai*.

Where do Japanese people find their *ikigai*? Apparently your *ikigai* lies at the centre of four interconnecting circles:

- mission: what you love
- vocation: what the world needs
- profession: what you can get paid for
- passion: what you're good at

Here is the challenge: perhaps it is easy to know your *ikigai* when you are just out of college and have a degree in your hand. The ink is wet and disappointment is a concept rather than a repeatedly lived experience. But what happens as you get older? How does a 30-year-old mother of two who is tied to the daily grind and can't get her head around what could actually make her happy find her *ikigai* beyond her kids? How does a woman in her 40s pursue her passion after a redundancy? Will it be financially viable?

Are you tied down by a mortgage or private school fees? Do you feel you are not good enough to pursue your passion? How do you get up and keep on running? How do you manage through the transitions?

Here is an important question: what is worse than the feeling that time is running out? It is the feeling that time *has* run out.

What does this look like? We are physically alive but the drive is gone and the vision is dulled, dimmed or, worse, dead. The dream is buried six feet under. We are just surviving, barely. If you want to live your life to the fullest with true purpose then start thinking about what sits at the centre of your four concentric circles.

You do not retire from your calling, you retire from your job.

If you think rediscovering, renewing and recommitting to an evolving purpose, passion and mission gets harder as you get older, think again. You need a mindset shift to see ageing as a privilege and an opportunity.

Clarissa Pinkola Estés wrote in *Women Who Run with the Wolves*: 'There are a lot of late bloomers among women. And women who are in their thirties, forties and fifties . . . who have never put their hand to the thing that their heart and soul says that would be interesting, exciting and fulfilling for them, it is never ever too late to blossom.' But can we allow ourselves to bloom later in life? Blooming means we will be seen and visible to a group that may only be used to us being invisible. This requires courage and is another step on the Courageous Path.

With a much longer life, can we slow down and master the art of multiple careers and multiple significant romantic relationships and incarnations of ourselves? Are we courageous enough to do this? Can we step into big transitions in life and navigate the changes asked of ourselves? Can we jump off one cliff with no feet on any solid foundation and believe we will not only land safely but where we are meant to? Do we instead worry about what other people will think and tell ourselves: 'We are too old. It's just too late. I don't want to make any more mistakes. Time has run out.'

Much like the black sheep syndrome, there is a syndrome called 'it's-too-late syndrome'. This is an invisible syndrome that is not spoken out loud but we have absorbed unquestioningly. If this is just a story we have told ourselves, can we untell it? How do you transition between the life to which you are resigned to a life of greater possibilities when you have financial and emotional obligations or commitments to grown-ups and little people?

We are all meant to experience a birth of some kind in our lifetime, whether it is a child, business, book, song, concept or a healed and whole version of ourselves. Not only that, we are meant to continue to birth, evolve and rebirth. When we do birth it is infused with a vibration of love; that is the feminine way. The only rule is to be authentic to ourselves. We can't start birthing early enough, and we don't stop birthing because we have become older.

Your purpose does not have a deadline or an expiry date. Your calling withstands the test of time.

VIVIENNE: NEVER TOO OLD OR YOUNG

Beauty begins the moment you decide to be yourself.

COCO CHANEL

'Sheila, I am moving to LA. I am going to live in America, I am going to meet someone, I am going to fall in love, I am going to get married and have a television show in America.' Vivienne is a professional make-up artist who had just turned 55. Against all Western preconceptions, she decided to take a leap. Does this sound unbelievable to you, or scoff-worthy? Did Vivienne have the dreams of a 21-year-old? Your dreams are your business alone and no one else's, and your *ikigai* has no number or age attached to it.

Vivienne had been doing make-up her whole life; it was her passion. In fact, she started out doing make-up for Australian celebrities such as Kylie Minogue when they were in their 20s and featured on iconic Australian television shows such as *Neighbours* and *Home and Away*. In a conversation about her courageous decision, Vivienne described a concept I have never heard of but one she was passionate about: 'We all have to face it: a beauty death. No woman escapes it.'

I knew what she was talking about. Still sensual, blonde and pretty, Vivienne felt she was experiencing her own beauty death, or the perceived death of her physical beauty as measured by conventional standards. This death meant that Vivienne was in a state of transition and it was an invitation to relook at her *ikigai*: her reason to get up in the morning.

On the Courageous Path we must be willing to let go of an aspect of ourselves that served us up to a point. This isn't just about our physical beauty; the beauty death will affect us all, but perhaps we will also have the marital death, the corporate career death, the motherhood death or the start-up business death. The death may also be the way we walk in the world: the death of our masculine or feminine self or the death of our physical strength.

When we embrace letting go of something we stand in the possibility of birthing something new and more aligned with where we are on the Courageous Path. Vivienne would later find that what she had gone through was not a beauty death at all but a beauty rebirth. We are always being called to realign with our changing selves, and perhaps the gestation period may be shorter or may last for much longer than nine months.

For Vivienne it took nine years to birth the next stage of her life: 'Timing and patience is everything. Patience, but not letting go of the dream. Too many of my girlfriends think "I'm older now" or 'It's too late." I lost one year of my three-year visa because I had to stay in Australia when my mother's health was ailing. I also decided to spend an extra year with my son because he was too young for me to leave. Despite all of this, you have to have your own dreams. But you also need patience and consistency to bring them into reality.'

Vivienne was passionate about helping women with ageing: 'There are people out there who know the secrets to earning wealth. There are people out there who know the secrets to marketing. I know the secret to maintaining a beauty that is mind, body and soul. A beauty that is still alluring, that is graceful for the age you're at.'

Vivienne had dedicated her life to understanding the mind, body and spirit and wanted to share her message with a larger group of people: 'I operate from a space of beliefs and an absolute belief where it's like I'm not even going to listen to me saying "Maybe not." It is my driving force.'

Perhaps we can learn from Vivienne how to rebirth ourselves. Perhaps moving to a new foreign city at an older age has kept Vivienne young and has built resilience and courage. She has had to be creative with solutions; she has had to let go and surrender. How much harder is it to surrender as we get older?

In this day and age of immediacy we often hear or see other people's stories and believe they have become successful without any setbacks. Vivienne's story dispels this notion: 'When I first moved to America I felt like I'd gone back to living like I was in my twenties. I was in a guest house and I had no independence. As a woman in my fifties I found that really disheartening. Even though the person I was living with was fine, I felt that I was taking a major step back in my life. But I told myself: "Just give it a couple of months." I was getting into a really negative space and thinking a lot of negative thoughts. I was even considering going home. I decided to sit in faith and I went to a meditation course for a month.

'Each week I sat down and meditated on being able to find my own place. I knew that there must have been a reason for being in my current situation. I ended up getting my own first apartment because of the year I spent living in that apartment block. It's hard getting a lease here in America, and because they all knew me personally and they liked me and trusted me I cut through all the red tape. I also met my husband in this apartment block.'

In her search for her *ikigai* Vivienne found love and a new life in a new country. She and her husband are halfway through shooting a pilot for her anti-ageing show. Vivienne's Courageous Path is one long interesting journey.

Vivienne didn't get lucky: she got courageous. She is still smack bang in the middle of her Courageous Path at the age of 57. She loves her work in LA and she is still pursuing her *ikigai*. Her courageous act was moving to a new country and pursuing her passion. Regardless of the ending of the story, Vivienne is an inspiration to women as she dared to colour outside the lines of her life. In walking her own Courageous Path, Vivienne has learned how to manage the big life transitions and, in doing so, has birthed a new phase of her life.

What have you wanted to birth for years?

NO REGRETS

What would You have me do? Where would You have me go? What would You have me say, and to whom?

HELEN SCHUCMAN

Bronnie Ware, author of *The Top Five Regrets of the Dying*, went in search of a job with meaning and found herself working in palliative care. While she sat with the dying she documented their thoughts, dreams and aspirations right before they left their physical body. She found that the number one regret of the dying was 'I wish I'd had the courage to live a life true to myself, not the life others expected of me.' This documented regret is not surprising, as what Bronnie states is something we all ache for. Having this desire and actually living into the truth of it before death comes knocking requires great courage.

NATALIE: A LIFE OF NO REGRETS

Your soul doesn't care what you do for a living – and when your life is over, neither will you. Your soul cares only about what you are being while you are doing whatever you are doing.

– NEALE DONALD WALSCH

Natalie Faber-Castell had found mastery in a life with no regrets. She was at the stage on her Courageous Path where she understood what living a life of no regrets looked like, yet this had not always been the way.

Natalie was born into a life of expectations. As a member of the well-known Faber-Castell family there was an expectation she would work in the family business. Perhaps this expectation was internally generated: sometimes it isn't just our surname that binds us to a life path we may be forced to consider. Our ancestral lineage, cultural influences and parents can have a far greater influence than we may allow ourselves to believe.

My father was a doctor and I remember asking myself: 'Do I want to be a doctor?' If my father wasn't a doctor, perhaps that question would never have been asked. An external reference point can make us question who we are. Perhaps it gives us a life path to resist and push against or a life path to submit to and be supported by.

What questions have you asked yourself that have determined the direction of your life? Have these questions served you?

Natalie did end up working in the family business; however, her journey did not end there. When she realised she was asking herself questions that were directly tied to her family and the expectations around her she decided to stop asking those questions and start living in the moment. She went on to carve out an eclectic career as a sound healer and musician.

What does life look like when you stop asking those questions and start living in the moment? Natalie is an example of someone living a life in flow; 'I surrender' was her daily internal mantra. How did Natalie make the transition? Moving away from the life she thought she was meant to live required a new way of thinking. She asked herself: 'Is there something better out there? I don't know what it is, but perhaps the universe will show me.' When we surrender we stop fighting against the life we are resistant to living.

I have discovered that when your life is all planned and doesn't work out it opens your mind to a better life that has not been planned out. That is the magic of surrender. The moment you stop trying to master your life and be in control is the moment you actually reach mastery.

Natalie said: 'The greatest things I have been involved in have literally fallen into my lap. I am a busy mother of two and running a part-time business, so I don't usually go to sound bath healings myself. I heard about this sound bath taking place. I listened to the voice that said "Stop doing the housework and go." Randomly going to this event changed my life. I just loved the way this organisation worked, so at the end I went up to the organiser and asked to be part of future projects. It was just so easy.'

As Natalie talked about this moment that shifted her thinking I reflected on how many times I have chased and hunted down my corporate goals, forcibly achieving them and not giving up regardless of how many doors were slammed shut in my face. Being out of flow with life felt hard and unfamiliar. When life is hard, dreams stop feeling like dreams and more like unattainable goals and we don't feel as though the universe has our back. When I started working as a medium and honouring what I knew I was meant to do with my life, the doors of unexpected experiences opened. A life of no regrets means stepping into these experiences and away from the expected experiences we think our life should contain.

The doors of unexpected experiences opened for Natalie too:'The organisation I had approached worked in palliative care hospitals. I *never* thought I would work with the terminally ill. It felt like such a privilege to be sharing a space with them. It is usually just for close family, so being there as a witness at the end of their life was such a unique experience.

'There was one time someone passed away while I was playing my sound healing bowls for them. He chose to let go in that moment as I was singing. Apparently he had been holding on for a long time. I knew this man still wanted music. You still want to have your senses nurtured and fed right up to the last breath. There is still life within you. He passed away in the first half of the first verse I was singing. I didn't know what the protocol was in this instance; I had never experienced anything like this. So I just kept singing.

'His daughter whispered: "He is gone." They were passing the tissues around and it felt right to finish the whole song. Nothing prepared me for this situation. It changed my view of life and the process of dying. Now I see the dying as still people in a body having a human experience even when they are dying. Right up to your last breath your human experience is still valid. You are still living.'

On the Courageous Path we need to be open to a place of continuous learning and inviting in new experiences. The path of courage continues to teach us, possibly in the most unexpected and unorthodox ways. The conservative, predictable and planned life will not teach us in the ways a surrendered life will. We must be open to the unexpected opportunities that arise in the small windows that open for us.

The Courageous Path involves letting life mould you and your outlook on life.

COURAGEOUS TRUTHS

1. On the Courageous Path your task is to discover your unique gifts and how to share them.

2. Your life has given you unique experiences, knowledge or lessons. You are required to reflect on this wisdom and pay it forward.

3. Women will birth and rebirth in their life; this cycle never ends. Your purpose has no end date.

4. Your *ikigai* is your reason to get up in the morning: what you love doing, what the world needs, what you can get paid for, what you are good at. It is your task to discover this for yourself.

5. The Courageous Path means having no regrets. Be open to the unexpected experiences and opportunities offered to you.

GET CURIOUS QUESTIONS

1. What qualities and gifts do your friends and family admire in you? (You may need to ask them this.)

2. What stands out from your childhood as unusual or interesting?

3. Can you recall a childhood, family or cultural experience in which you felt like an outsider or outcast? How might this experience relate to your larger purpose?

4. Is there an unfulfilled dream in your life? Do you feel like you are too old or that time has run out for you? If the perceived judgement from your family and friends was absent, would you do it?

5. What mindset change could allow you to be more in flow with the universe? How can you be more spontaneous and open to opportunities?

POWER PHRASE

'I honour my gifts and wisdom and I share my gifts and wisdom with the world.'

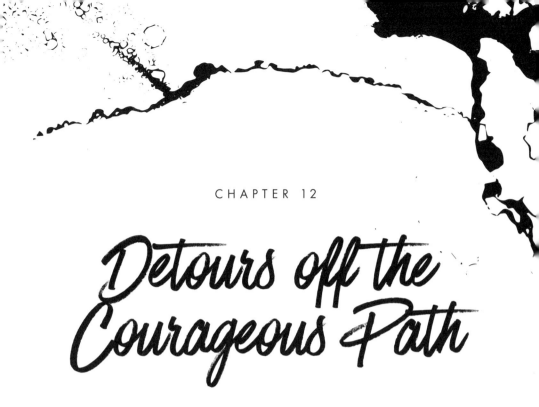

CHAPTER 12

Detours off the Courageous Path

Don't dance around the perimeter
of the person you want to be.

– GABRIELLE BERNSTEIN

STANDING IN THE SHADOW OF ANOTHER

Julia Cameron, author of *The Artist's Way,* describes how 'Shadow Artists often choose shadow careers – those close to the desired art, even parallel to it, but not the art itself.' Your job or career may look and present as though it is your calling: voluntary service work, protesting for a meaningful cause, attending workshop after workshop to transform your mind and body, wondering when you will be healed, whole and complete. Cameron says: 'Shadow artists are gravitating to their rightful tribe but cannot yet claim their birthright.' Your soul knows these activities are not your very own dream but are a surrogate for or distractions from your own calling. Even if they feel related, if you are not directly engaged in your own calling and purpose a dissatisfaction will soon begin to build.

When Alice Cheng started Coffee with a CFO the business was a part-time calling: she juggled a household that involved a corporate job and two young children. I didn't think twice when she reached out to me to participate in her mentoring event. Alice and I were in the minority of women who had made it to the financial C suite: you may not be surprised to know that only 12 per cent of CFOs globally are women (Korn Ferry, 2019). It was a thorny passage to the top for both of us, and we were at a point in our careers where we wanted to share the lessons we had learned from both the corporate traps and triumphs experienced.

A month later I sat around a table with a group of eight wide-eyed women who worked in accounting. They bucked the stereotype: they were sassy, dynamic and eager to be mentored.

On the Courageous Path you will be called to inspire others. As I sat and talked to these woman, most of whom I would never see again, I knew some of my words would stay with them. I also knew that in speaking my wisdom, failures and vulnerabilities I would awaken them to their own truths about themselves. As we climb ahead on the Courageous Path we need to look back and help those behind us: it is as much a fuel for them as it is for ourselves. We forget where we have come from, where our journey began. As I spoke I realised the significance of each step of my own journey, but when I left the group of women another thing happened.

An unexpected feeling washed over me: I felt like a fraud. I had just asked these women to display more courage in their lives, yet was I the most courageous version of myself? Although I was a participant in Coffee with a CFO I was not ready to step into my own soul work, which was being a spiritual teacher and medium. Was I being a shadow artist? I was not willing or courageous enough to give my own soul calling 100 per cent of my time and energy, so I allowed myself to get distracted. I supported women like Alice with their big audacious callings because of course I wanted to support Alice, but I also knew I was avoiding taking my own next courageous steps.

We can trick our soul, but only temporarily. Following someone else's purpose tricks our soul into thinking we are living our own purpose, because it can *feel* like we are. When we follow someone else's Courageous Path we do feel courageous ourselves: why wouldn't we? As women we swarm in tribes and are inspired and inspiring to one another. Perhaps it is a distraction from the serious commitment required to follow our own path? Sometimes our personal mission isn't completely understood and we are in training; we feel good following the inspiration of another soul sister. Yes, together we rise, but we must also feed our own soul first and at some point our soul will ask us to put ourselves first.

ALICE: PERIOD PANTIES AND PURPOSE

I tried quitting sugar once. I dropped a heap of weight, a heap of purpose and a heap of friends, and I wanted to punch a vegan.

CELESTE BARBER

Period panties are reusable and sustainable leak-proof underwear that replace the need for tampons, pads and incontinence products. I love this underwear. As I sit writing this paragraph I am in day three of my moon cycle and I am wearing a pair: they are sexy and 100 per cent leak-proof. Yet when my friend Alice said she was changing jobs and joining a company that sold period underwear full time as a director, I must admit I screwed my face up and revealed my opinion a little too quickly: 'What about your *own* business, Coffee with a CFO? You are so passionate about helping women in finance.'

'That can wait. I am not ready to commit to my business full time.'

Working at this company ticked some big boxes for Alice. Most women use around 11,000 disposable menstrual products in their lifetime and around 90 per cent of those products are made of plastic. This was a company that was passionate about empowering women and reducing landfill: sounds like the stuff of soul purpose work, right? It was, but it wasn't Alice's soul purpose work. It was a pit stop. If we need to take a pit stop as a shadow artist that is okay; however, it is just that: a pit stop and a time of preparation. Another step around the corner was waiting silently and patiently for Alice.

Time spent as a shadow artist can be a time of preparation. It can be a training ground, as when you step up to your calling much will be asked of you: sacrifice, focus, resilience and commitment. It does take time to build these emotional muscles. We must also recognise that we are getting close to our purpose but not fully embodying it.

When Alice joined the company there was a niggle that started to churn in her belly. Avoidance of your purpose makes you feel less vulnerable in the short term, but this doesn't last. The niggle in Alice's belly would not go away. Twelve months later she left her job. She still loved the concept of period underwear but, like me, she needed to break away from serving others in order to serve herself.

She later said to me: 'My purpose is to help one person at a time, whether it is in their career or with their confidence. I found that for many of my clients their managers were not coaching them or they just did not know their path to become a CFO. So I really had to help them believe that they could. To help them believe that they could get there too.

'In running my own business I have felt alone when I have had months where I have not hit my sales target. I've thought: "Gosh, should I give up?" Then I've gone back to the testimonials from people on social media. I've read them one by one. And slowly my faith has returned that this is what I am meant to do. I have felt inspired again. I do think in those moments: "I have changed someone's life."'

With this inspiration as a driving force, Alice is now helping women climb this particular ladder and is creating a tribe of CFOs around her to support. Period stains on underwear, once a taboo topic, is now getting some visual social media time. Check out #happyperiods, #pinkbits, #bloodygoodperiod and #goauntflow. Spirituality, psychics and mediums and tarot and crystals are also becoming more accepted, yet as a group of women, perhaps individually, we still hide our period stains. We also don't openly talk about our spiritual nature, intuitive abilities or experiences unless we feel safe. And we definitely don't openly discuss the deepest desires of our soul.

You can follow the group and stand in the shadow of a soul sister for a while. Sometimes there is a time where you do need to observe and learn from those further ahead of you on the Courageous Path. You may think you are learning technical skills, but really you are learning how to be courageous. When you step up, also know there is a group that will follow you.

A year later I attended another Coffee with a CFO event. During the event Alice and I shared a knowing smile about what we had both sacrificed and the time we had waited to understand what it took to finally honour ourselves. Perhaps the women we were speaking to would follow this path, a path we had swept a little smoother for them.

Are you standing in the shadow or the light of your purpose?

ANGIE: GETTING BUMPED BACK ONTO THE PATH

When one is pretending, the entire body revolts.

ANAÏS NIN

We must let life bump us along when we get off track. We are allowed to get lost when we are trying to find ourselves and our greater purpose. The smell, taste and sounds of old habits and patterns may keep on pulling us back to a previous version of ourselves. Maybe our lessons have only been partially learned and we need reminders until the lessons are fully learned and integrated into our life. Because of this we will encounter bumps.

Bumps are not dark nights but they can still feel uncomfortable. The magic happens when you see them as small course corrections, like a sailing boat tacking its course. It is actually very hard to sail in a straight line, as the wind is unpredictable. When sailing you need to respond by sailing into the wind: much like life.

Angie Cowen, the founder of Love Life and Gluten Free, has a story about listening to your body: 'It was a year of tonsillitis, glandular fever, anxiety and depression. It was a full body shut down. The doctors put me on eight rounds of antibiotics. I got to the point where I thought this is just not working, so I needed to look to other factors. I started paying attention to what I was putting into my mouth, and then slowly also what I was feeding my mind. Gluten, dairy and sugar impacted my energy levels, so when I removed them from my diet my tonsillitis went straight away. I have been on the biggest journey to heal myself. Fifteen years ago no one was doing gluten free; I had to figure this all out on my own. So I did.'

Angie became an expert, not just on gluten-free cooking but on a disciplined approach to her physical and mental health. She launched a series of gluten-free products and two gluten-free cookbooks and has opened a health retreat centre: 'The universe would bump me back onto my path every time I strayed from taking care of my mental or physical health. I would get sick. The thing with my physical constitution was that I wouldn't just get a little sick, I would feel really awful then I would get anxious and depressed. Because the symptoms were so strong and my commitment to feeling good was even stronger, I started to make the changes and be consistent with them.'

In *The Body is the Barometer of the Soul* Annette Noontil noted: 'Disease does not bring pain. The pain of your soul brings disease. Pain is good because it gives you the idea that you need to look into yourself. Use the pain.'

Depression, anxiety and ill-health are feedback from our body that parts of our life are not working. When we listen to the feedback we can harness the knowledge we already have and allow ourselves to be bumped back along the path. Angie did not make herself wrong; she watched how she responded, and until she had mastery she allowed the universe to course correct her to full vitality.

Are you listening to your body? What is the experience of your periods?
How do you feel when you wake up?
Do you have aches?
Your body is speaking to you.

PIP: FAILURE IS AN IMPORTANT PART OF A SUCCESSFUL LIFE

Learning how to fail will help us more than anything else in life.
PEMA CHÖDRÖN

The courageous make mistakes. A lot of them. Learning to fail is a critically important part of the Courageous Path, yet being successful in our minds can create an absolute aversion to failing. When you are a perfectionist, failure is something of a tough sell. How can both co-exist? They need to. Mastery comes from learning to be with the shame and humiliation that can occur during the experience of failing and then gaining insight quickly.

Bestselling author Pip Drysdale epitomised that. She had written almost 90,000 words for her second book, but as she pressed send and delivered her final manuscript to her publisher she had a laser-sharp gut instinct. She knew this next book had been written with her head and not her heart. She had a big intuitive and creative heart and she understood her craft; this was not her best writing.

Soon after her publisher called her and agreed. Pip recalls she was actually relieved. When we met I was holding Pip's second book – the one that did get published, *The Strangers We Know*. It had a killer story line, pacing plot, seductive heartbreak and saucy men. 'Didn't you feel like an utter failure when the previous manuscript got rejected? All that wasted time, an entire year writing a book for nothing?' I asked her. I was projecting my own experience on to her. I knew that *I* would have felt like a big, fat flop if that had happened to me.

Pip pushed my projection back. 'Not at all! I just thought: "Screw it, I am going to start again – new plot, new character, new everything." I wrote the next book in four and a half months, and I couldn't have written that book without writing the one before. So none of the time was wasted. It was a way of honing my skills and getting better. So, yes, it might have looked like a rejection, but the truth is every writer has at least one manuscript that didn't quite work sitting in a drawer somewhere. It's part of the process.'

Pip had mastered the mindset of being okay to fail, which is why success eventually found its way to her. Not only that, she saw the gift in the setback. The book she wrote next was a better book for the failure.

During nearly 15 years in the publishing industry I saw this countless times: the dreaded disappointing second book syndrome (DSBS), which is an actual syndrome and doesn't *just* occur within the book publishing industry. It also applies to life. Sometimes we want life to be a continual conga line of awards, applauses, promotions and successful relationships, or we may be so scared of failing that we just don't take any steps forward. We don't ever write the second book.

Current success in any aspect of our life does not guarantee continued success. If we demand a continual flow of success we become less resilient to failure. It is exhausting trying to succeed and is how we get burnt out. Failure takes us into a state of reflection where we pause, and during the pause we evolve and new wisdom is integrated. We are then ready for our next stage of growth.

Expectations of success also kill creativity. We must always love what we do. If Pip had focused on the destination to get a second fiction bestseller written, the rejection of her 90,000 words would have had her collapse in a screaming heap. Instead she didn't go into shame when she received the call.

When we don't go into shame all our senses can switch on – especially our sixth sense – and be ready to receive critical information. This means we start to listen and see things more clearly, enabling us to kick into a learning process quickly. We stand a chance to pick ourselves up off the floor, dust ourselves off and move forward with greater insight.

It is important to learn from failure, but we must allow ourselves to fail first.

Turn the alchemy of rejection, perceived failure or a setback into something more powerful. The universe is always working with us to ensure we are on track. Learning to see that we are on track is a very powerful thought we can hold.

As Pip wisely says: 'If you love what you are doing there is no failing. It just doesn't exist.'

We are quick to see success; social media has trained us to do so. Behind the screen of success we don't see the struggle, the learnings, the failures that really are essential. Social media ensures we don't see these: it is not selfie time when we pack our belongings and are fired from our job; it is not selfie time when we decide to quit our marriage. But when we look at other people's fabulous Insta stories we create our own internal Insta story that a life of success is easy, instant and continuous and sometimes beyond our own reach.

As I scrolled down Pip's social media feed I was watching the many photos of her book tour. There was no evidence of the rejected manuscript. I am glad I knew the backstory. Pip didn't need to share this private experience with everyone; it was her private experience. We all have private experiences of failure, but learning to truly take wisdom from them is the mastery we seek on the Courageous Path.

THE GURU BOYFRIEND SYNDROME

Love yourself first and everything else falls into line. You really have to love yourself to get anything done in this world.
LUCILLE BALL

Self-sacrifice is a quick route off your Courageous Path. When you start walking on someone else's path, years later you will wonder: 'How did I get here? Is it too late to go back?' We don't mean to veer off our path and onto someone else's. Sometimes this change happens over a long time and we don't realise it is happening. We wake up one day and ask ourselves: 'Whose life am I living?'

On a third date with a dashing lawyer I was chanting out loud the name of Krishna. My eyes were shut, and I was sitting on a bright orange frayed pillow and draped in a borrowed orange shawl. A part of me was in awe, a part of me had already fallen in love and a part of me was terrified that I had joined some sort of cult. At the end of two hours of a group chanting meditation called a *satsang* I recall thinking: 'How am I going to tell my parents I am now a Hare Krishna?' My boyfriend had a guru in India and his social tribe in Sydney were all devotees. I immediately joined the gang.

As I child I knew the Hare Krishnas were an enigmatic clan of people who sang and swayed their hips and merged two opposite cultures. Collectively they were just a little too happy and a little too orange. As a sensitive child I could feel the discomfort everyone felt as this group of men and women danced and chanted their way through the streets of Sydney.

After falling in love with this guru-following lawyer boyfriend I spent a year reading Vedic teachings and devoting myself to 10 hours a week of chanting meditation. I did this because I was in love, and love can make you do crazy and obsessive things to seek approval and acceptance. Self-sacrifice was the dragon tattoo on my lower back, a permanent feature of my romantic relationships. I was an ultra chameleon. Chameleons do not change their colour to blend in with their surroundings; in fact, for most chameleons changing colours is all about finding a mate. 'You love Krishna? Wow, so do I!' I was after a husband and enlightenment at the same time so I thought I had hit the Kama Sutra jackpot.

After a year we were the ultimate conscious couple. The next milestone was flying to India to meet my partner's guru. I think that was one of the early red flags waving furiously at me: the guru was not my guru but my partner's guru, but I hadn't foreseen the problem as I was counting down the days to go. A week before I was due to go something happened.

He died.

Not my boyfriend; the guru. He was 92 years old. When I received the news I was devastated as I had wanted to meet this master. Having watched hundreds of hours of his teachings I was in awe of this man but, most importantly, my relationship was riding on meeting him. No contact with the guru meant no commitment of marriage to this man – or so I thought.

This is what self-sacrifice looks like: you give up your own spiritual truths, your diet (I was now vegetarian), your own morning ritual (I was now waking up at five a.m. to meditate) and Netflix (my partner insisted on a ban on television). Season six of *Game of Thrones* had just been released and everyone was talking about it. I was desperate to watch it. My boyfriend was not controlling; it was just that I was a goddess of self-sacrifice. When a suggestion was offered to me within this relationship I would bow my head and subjugate: not all the time, but enough that I became lost. Very lost.

The destination of self-sacrifice is lost.

We broke up a year later. If you self-sacrifice in a relationship it is very hard to stop once you start. I did not know how to reclaim my power.

The journey to meet the guru was actually a journey to meet my inner guru. I had made my partner the guru: I had kissed the soles of his feet and self-sacrificed for two full years. I had made him constantly right and myself constantly wrong. Sometimes you need to give all your love away to return to love within yourself.

When you detour off the Courageous Path the journey back is through self-love. There is no self-love mountain to climb. Self-love is not a quest and is not found at the end of a pilgrimage, so don't run away looking for it. Self-love is a lived experience and is made up of constant daily actions. Like yoga, it is a practice, not a destination. Self-love begins with self; you cannot find self-love in anyone else. The practice of self-love is to continually come back to the heart and mind of self.

I could tell you to take a rose petal bath, get a massage or light a beautiful scented candle as an act of self-love, but this is not *you* talking to *you*. It is another external ritual that you need to question: 'Am I honouring myself if I do this?' Daily rituals are the difference between a good life and a great life, and these rituals need to honour the self. You need to find your way to the daily rituals that honour you. With repetition these rituals strengthen your understanding of what feels good in your life and what does not.

You may still lose yourself on someone else's Courageous Path, but with awareness of self-love you will not walk as long on their path. You will miss your acts of self-love and you will notice the feelings far sooner when your life starts to feel as if it veering off course because you have taught yourself what it feels like to have a life that is on course. Sometimes, getting lost is the journey back to self-love. The reclamation of your self-love can only be achieved after losing it and being in a lot of pain. I do not know of any pain greater than the one I have inflicted on myself by not loving myself enough.

After my break up I would still wake up at five every morning, but instead of meditating I binge-watched *Game of Thrones*: I had seven seasons to catch up on. The Courageous Path involves honouring yourself and that, at times, may involve binge-watching Netflix.

Years later I was coaching a client who was desperately searching for a guru in India. She mentioned that a lot of people were trying to dissuade her from going and asked for my opinion, but my opinion wasn't the point. I asked her three questions:

- What are you looking to learn?
- Who are you seeking to find?
- If I said 'Don't go', would you stay?

A month later my client left for India. We must all travel on our own Courageous Path to find our own inner guru who will teach us self-love. The path will no doubt include detours. Perhaps this is the path itself? Our task is to find our inner guru, and you may have to meet a couple of outer gurus, teachers and masters along the way to get there.

COURAGEOUS TRUTHS

1. Beware of spending too long training for your purpose, as you may in fact be hiding from your purpose.

2. Your body is constantly speaking to you. When you are on track you will feel energised and when you are off track you may experience illness.

3. Mastering failure is an important part of mastering courage.

4. Let self-sacrifice teach you only once. Learn the lesson and then powerfully move forward on your Courageous Path.

GET CURIOUS QUESTIONS

1. How long are you willing to delay stepping into your purpose?

2. What are you learning by supporting someone else's purpose?

3. What will it take for you to feel ready to step into your purpose? Perhaps you are ready now?

4. Think back to a time when you felt and decided you were not good enough. What advice would you give your younger self?

5. If you could not fail, what would you do now?

6. What message, information and feelings do your body repeatedly give you? Do you listen?

7. What is the biggest failure you have experienced in your life personally? What have you learned from this experience?

8. Where are you sacrificing yourself in your romantic relationships and how might this be a detour from your purpose?

9. Who do you give your power away to: at work, in relationships, in your family?

10. Describe a healthy balanced romantic relationship and your behaviour in this relationship.

POWER PHRASE

'I am enough, I am worthy, I am loveable. I lead myself back onto my Courageous Path.'

CHAPTER 13

What it takes

The Courageous Path is available to everyone. Whether a person decides to venture into its different terrains depends on whether they have what it takes. You will be called to set fear aside and embrace opportunities you feel unprepared for. You will be called to not quit when your mind screams 'bolt now'. The path will feel like the course of a marathon: long and unforgiving. You will need to be unreasonable in your requests from those around you to create miraculous opportunities. You will need to allow things to unfold and be fuelled by passion. Most importantly, you will need the courage to think for yourself, to make the choices only you can make. This requires great self-belief.

SAYING YES BEFORE YOU THINK YOU ARE READY

Just say yes and you'll figure it out afterward.

TINA FEY

Saying yes before you are ready is an act of courage.

My mentor suggested I was ready to go on *Psychic TV*. I gasped. 'What? There is *no* way I am going on live television.' We had a lengthy conversation about it. *Psychic TV* was broadcast live to an Australian audience and involved doing on-air psychic and mediumship readings. During the conversation with my mentor I did most of the talking and my language was filled with words like 'can't', 'won't' and 'no'. When I wasn't jabbering on in resistance I was silent and fearful. 'What if I make a fool of myself?'

My mentor listened patiently as I catastrophised different scenarios. I received an email a few days later from the television network letting me know I would be on air in two weeks. I panicked.

When we are requested to step up onto our Courageous Path our job is to short circuit the neural pathway in the brain that immediately responds with a 'no': our reptilian brain. The one that is keeping us safe. The one that is also keeping us bored and stuck. The questions we ask ourselves are important when we are invited by the universe to step up. It can be the difference between a yes or a 'no', the difference between a life-changing experience or standing on the precipice of fear waiting for optimum weather conditions. I asked myself when would I feel ready? Would I ever feel ready? If not now then when?

Entrepreneur Jim Rohn says: 'There are two types of pain you will go through in life: the pain of discipline and the pain of regret. Discipline weighs ounces, while regret weighs tons.' I knew I did not want to carry the heavy weight of a 'no' with me. I was at a point on my Courageous Path where I had taken many leaps of courage and had survived numerous dark nights of courage. The signs that I was on the right track were bountiful.

When I paused and answered these questions something happened: a switch flicked in my brain. I asked: 'Who am I to not do this?' I agreed to the offer.

I realised the universe had given me this opportunity and I needed to recognise that. This opportunity would not have come up if I was not ready. Sometimes the opportunities come to us and we don't feel ready. We have created a thought, a vision and a desire and then the actual thing we want shows up, but in our minds the timing is off. The truth is the timing is 100 per cent right and we just need to work through the fear-based doubts that are holding us back.

I dropped the panic and shifted my focus to preparation. Why? Because I had a deadline, because I had a commitment I had to honour.

Fear can be useful when we lasso it into submission, stare it in the eyes and ask: 'What are you showing me?' My fear was showing me I was not entirely prepared for the experience of going on Australian television. My fear showed me there were some gaps in my knowledge I needed to bridge, so I searched for someone to teach me. The courageous act of saying yes can spur us into an action that keeps fear at a social distance and makes us untouchable, allowing us to be focused on our goal.

A week later I was in rehearsal in front of a camera in a small studio. I didn't have enough money to pay for the crew. The courage to say yes invites other creative steps, so I put a proposition to the camerawoman: 'I can pay you half the price and I will give free on-camera intuitive and mediumship readings to you and three of your staff. You just need to give me feedback about my accuracy. How does that sound?' She had never had an offer like that before but she agreed. When you say yes to the universe people around you also start saying yes.

How did this story end? In the lead up to the show I was a nervous wreck: even though I had lassoed and tamed fear it was still there. The host, a familiar face to her fans, confidently turned to the camera and introduced me. In that moment I was live on Australian television doing psychic and mediumship readings for the viewers who called in. Going on television was not the act of courage; it was saying yes when I was asked. A wave of calm settled into my body as the show proceeded. When we say yes we can then take action to practise, prepare and perform.

The Courageous Path doesn't end with this Courageous Leap, with the yes. It is a long continual road of yes. When we practise saying yes we build up this muscle and also build skills, expertise, resilience and courage. We begin to embrace uncertainty and learn not to run from it. The Courageous Path is one of learning and growth: saying yes before you are ready isn't easy, but to walk courageously forward it is a required step. Our future yes will eventually become past achievements, this is how the path is travelled.

The universe knows that you are ready, so just say 'Yes.'

THE 62,926 STEPS RULE

We covet the diamond and overlook the pressure it took to make it.

GREGG LEVOY

Did you know that women run a marathon in approximately 62,926 steps? Do you think a marathon runner knows this when their chest is on fire as they are running up a hill? Do you think a marathon runner even cares?

There are many blogs and tips about running marathons. When you start to train for a marathon you see the goal as crossing the finishing line, but success comes from persistent daily actions, discipline, enduring pressure and great sacrifices along the way. At this point on the Courageous Path your mindset has shifted and you are ready to make short-term sacrifices. You can see that sacrifice has a greater gain: the joy of being in action towards fulfilling your purpose. You are measured, calm and in action as you walk the Courageous Path.

The 62,926 steps are irrelevant. In training for a marathon, every day you focus on the program you are committed to doing that day. There is advice from the many marathon runners who have run before you that this is the program that will ensure success. The average marathon runner runs one million steps (gasp!) in the six months prior to a marathon. This is a staggering number, but that is the reality of the work that is needed to successfully get to the finish line. Very few marathon runners know or care about this. They wake up most mornings – heavy rain, blistering heat or gale-force winds – and train their pants off. They eat carefully to sustain their energy, they stretch their muscles and stop when injured, and they listen to their sporting gods (their physiotherapists) for a quick return to their disciplined routine. I used to be a runner, and for a while I was seeing my physiotherapist more than my parents or boyfriend.

After Kate quit the police force she got into action to open her yoga studio. She took quantum leaps. Witnessing her in action was like watching a dedicated woman train for a marathon. This was a whole new world for her (much like marathon running). She had been employed for over a decade and raised four kids. She didn't know about rental leases, social media marketing, shipping in yoga mats from China or sophisticated client-booking systems. But as with a marathon runner, each daily activity, phone call, business coffee or formal document filled out in triplicate was a step in her training.

Kate had taken her Courageous Leaps two years earlier and the repeated loop of self-doubting questions had ceased. She was now asking herself different questions. Practical questions that are not filled with emotions and self-doubt will move us into action quickly. If you are an accountant you will love these questions: they are all logic and no emotions, and sometimes that is what is needed. The emotions have been addressed and resolved and the big actions are what is now needed to create success. These actions create the changes in our life we seek. The daily actions Kate took not only guaranteed success but kept her anxiety low and her sense of mission fulfilled and real. Opening a yoga studio was no longer a dream in the future: it was a reality she was creating for herself in the moment.

As with marathon training, each step and big courageous action takes us closer to the success we desire. Sometimes we can sit in the morass of our emotions for too long and feel stuck. When we move into action it allows for mastery and control over our emotions and allows us to create the life and relationships we want.

When a marathon runner crosses the finishing line it doesn't matter what the spectators think. There is a smile of relief, accomplishment and knowledge that it took every blister, aching muscle and dawn start to successfully cross that line. It will have taken considerable preparation to break through new physical, mental and emotional barriers.

Your Courageous Path will at times require endurance and stamina.

KATH: NOT QUITTING SYNDROME

The hallmark of courage is knowledge and feeling, 'I can' . . . in this state we can be very effective in the world.

DAVID R. HAWKINS

We can start something but not have the grit to finish it. Success is the outcome of not quitting. When we finally reach our goal on the Courageous Path we think the hard work is behind us. When we arrive at the next significant stage we may be summoned to find a deeper level of commitment to our purpose. It is at this point we are required to work harder and find even more stamina, dedication and resolve. This is when your mettle will be truly tested, and this is why sometimes the destination of success comes a little later. During the time we are waiting for the red carpet to roll out we are being prepared to embody resilience and tenacity and our backbone is strengthened and straightened. We need these virtues in larger stores to sustain our purpose and must go through a process of maturing to be able to handle not only reaching but holding our dreams.

Kath had come a long way from the Tamworth Country Music Festival competition, busking on the London Tube and accepting gigs at any venue that would take her, whether it be Sydney, London or Los Angeles. She made success look easy, but she had a-not-quitting attitude and it paid off.

Kath said: 'When I found out my musical was accepted onto a London stage I felt really overwhelmed, to be honest. It was that moment when something you have worked so hard for and dreamed about for so long finally happens. On the day I found out I thought: "Today I have achieved my specific goal and this was what I was meant to do my whole entire life." But do you know what? You would expect it to be pure joy, but it wasn't. I felt excited and scared at the same time. I did not see this emotion coming.'

We don't believe our dreams will actualise, instead believing they will remain as a dream. But if you are focused and in alignment with your purpose and have the willpower to hunt down your dreams, there is a high probability you'll actually catch them. Then what? Have you even prepared for that? We can spend a long time on the Courageous Path looking for our purpose and chasing down significant milestones. When the vision, dream or pinnacle on the Courageous Path shows up do we have the strength and stamina to keep going, or are we caught off guard, our resolve weakening? Do we just run out of puff? Once we achieve our goal we open ourselves to a whole new level of responsibility.

Why don't we dream past the dream? Because we don't believe that the dream of accomplishing our life purpose will eventuate. So why look further ahead on the Courageous Path? Not quitting is about the persistent hard work required to reach milestones on our Courageous Path. Not quitting is also about not quitting dreaming.

Not quitting isn't about arriving at a destination: it is about keeping going. When you arrive at the destination you realise it is one of many destinations.

Expect to achieve to your dreams and then you will be called to dream again.

SHAUNA: BEING UNREASONABLE

Ask for what you want and be prepared to get it.

MAYA ANGELOU

When we are unreasonable with our requests it can alter the course of our life. What does being unreasonable mean? It means having the guts to make a bold request to the universe, family, friends or a stranger for help on our Courageous Path. It also means making a request and expecting a big, audacious, unequivocal yes as a reply.

At age 19 Dr Shauna Shapiro made an unreasonable request that changed the course of her life. I would like to say for the better, but there is no better. There is a knowing that brought her into alignment with her greater destiny and altered the course of her life towards the course she was meant to be on: 'When I was nineteen my dad gave me this book by Jon Kabat-Zinn, *Wherever You Go, There You Are*. I read it and reread it. It really changed my life.'

Remember that Shauna spent six months lying on her back after excruciating spinal surgery, so she began reaching for tools to help her with her daily pain management. 'This book was my first real introduction to mindfulness.' Something in Shauna's heart had been stirred, so what did she do? She listened to the stirrings of her heart and responded with an unreasonable request.

'I was living abroad in Israel and I was flying to Spain. On the plane trip I wrote Jon Kabat-Zinn this letter. I wrote: "Your book changed my life. This is what I want to do with my life. When I graduate from Duke and I'm back in the United States, can I please come and study with you?"'

'And four months later I get a letter in Spain from him. He said: "I was so moved by your letter. I read it to 500 people at a conference. Whenever you get back and after you graduate from college I'll give you a scholarship to come train with me in Massachusetts." And so as soon as I graduated, I went and trained with him.'

Our life is one long mala bead necklace of teachers, mentors and guides strung carefully together in perfect order. Our purpose in life is to reach for them, to unravel the necklace one bead at a time with courage and conviction. Shauna had just been to Thailand and had a synchronistic meeting with a monk, the first of her many teachers and way showers, to point to the next stepping stone on her path. Because of her unreasonable request, Jon Kabat-Zinn powerfully stepped forward as her next teacher.

Be unreasonable in your requests and you will be unreasonably rewarded.

Twenty years later Shauna published her bestselling book, *Good Morning, I Love You*, about the science and practice of self-kindness, the secret source of fulfilment, transformation and joy.

One wonders if Shauna would have written her book and given a TEDx talk that would change the lives of millions of people if she had not made that unreasonable request to study with Jon Kabat-Zinn all those years before. Shauna had allowed herself to act in the moment, to make an unreasonable request as a response to something that had a great impact on her. She didn't let the loud voice of doubt stop her. Her knowing at that point was that she wanted to explore this subject and perhaps help other people. This part was still unknown and uncharted. She didn't have aspirations of fame, but she did have aspirations to serve and live a life of meaning.

A courageous life asks us to be unreasonable. When our passions are met with unreasonable requests miracles occur.

Two years into my role as a finance director at Simon & Schuster, I made what I believed to be an unreasonable request of my boss: I asked to work four days a week. I wanted to go part time so I could pursue my spiritual career. For months I put off what felt like an impossible conversation. I was waiting for a no, I was expecting conflict and a combative argument. The many ways I had talked myself out of asking included justifying that no other finance director had worked part time before. I didn't think my staff would support me and thought my boss would be irritated and annoyed.

When you look for blockages to your unreasonable questions you will easily find them.

I had no evidence that any of those assumptions were right: it was fear-based thinking and it was keeping me stuck. One day the courage factor outweighed the fear factor, which is the formula for making an unreasonable request. I was feeling tormented at work, that I was facing another five-day work week with the two days of the weekend serving my spiritual clients.

I was on another road to burn out, and I found the conviction to make an unreasonable request.

Upon reflection, I had delayed a part of my life and I felt deprived. I had not considered that my boss could see my longing to transition into this part of my life. When I wasn't talking about work I loved to discuss anything spiritual with him. He wanted to keep me motivated at work, which involved helping me to be as authentic as possible. I just needed to summon up the courageous internal stores and make the request.

He said yes. Years later when I look back it seemed so much more of a reasonable request and that the universe through him was conspiring to help me. Unreasonable requests look unreasonable just because we don't make them often or see them made often.

When we don't make unreasonable requests we can remain stuck and delay living our authentic life.

TAKING TOTAL RESPONSIBILITY

Life becomes easier when you learn to accept the apology you never got.
ROBERT BRAULT

Healing can be instant or it can take a lifetime. I want to introduce you to a radical concept that clears negativity from your mind and thoughts but requires a powerful mindset of total responsibility. First I want to share a story with you. This story sounds like an urban myth but stick with me.

The criminally insane ward at Hawaii State Hospital was a tough place to work. Often new staff would only last one month and taking a sick day from work was a regular occurrence. Then a very special therapist came along. He was committed to treating the inmates … without ever seeing, speaking or touching them. No contact. His approach was radical and revolutionary – and it worked.

How did he do it? By assuming total responsibility, meaning he took responsibility for the actions of the inmates. He adopted a mindset that saw him being responsible for their injustices, their harms, their crimes, their prejudices. How did he do this? He was given an office at the hospital and he sat there by himself looking at their medical files one by one. With each inmate he looked within himself to see how he created that person's illness (yes, himself!). He took total responsibility for the inmates' mental illness.

The technique he used was the Ho'oponopono practice.

The therapist repeated the words 'I love you' and 'I am sorry' over and over again while reviewing each file. After a few months things started to change quite quickly. The patients who were bound by straightjackets and shackles were allowed to walk freely as their behaviour had dramatically improved. Patients had their medication reduced or were taken off their medications completely. Some cases that had shown no hope were eventually released back into society.

This process only took several months. The final cherry on the cake is that this mental ward is now closed. This is no urban myth: the man's name is Dr Ihaleakalā Hew Len. Inspirational speaker Joe Vitale brought his story to life in his book *Zero Limits*.

Ho'oponopono is an ancient spiritual practice of recitation of a mantra that originated in Hawaii and, before that, in the Polynesian islands of the South Pacific. It was used as a form of conflict resolution to help one island kingdom settle their differences with another. The mantra is:

I am sorry.
Please forgive me.
Thank you.
I love you.

The basis of the mantra comes from the one principle Hawaiians teach: *hurt no one*. We must be responsible for all our experiences in life, which is a core concept of Ho'oponopono. When we accept responsibility for our own experience we are then able to manifest and create the reality we really want. We can then truly create a harmonious work environment and improve interpersonal relationships with colleagues. When using this mantra you're speaking to the universal source. The idea is not to aim to change or fix another person or situation but to focus on yourself for healing. When you heal yourself, everything else in your reality will change.

I like doing experiments on myself. As a spiritual teacher I cannot teach a concept or methodology I have not experienced or one I don't believe in. I can admit I didn't believe the power of the Ho'oponopono prayer when I first heard the story. I had recited many different mantras and chants in my life and thought to myself: 'How can this mantra be so different and so powerful?'

One particular week I had quite a few clients who were holding on to resentments relating to their ex-partners and family members. When you work as a coach or mentor, sometimes themes cluster together to help you. In this instance I needed to learn the lesson that there was a greater way to serve my clients and a new tool was needed in my spiritual toolkit.

I decided to record a meditation to facilitate forgiveness in my clients. I recorded the Ho'oponopono prayer as a meditation of healing and recited the mantra 108 times to beautiful sacred music. It took 20 minutes. As I recorded the meditation I thought about all the people in my life who I loved and all the people I resented, and about people I felt poorly about as I had lost touch with them. As I recorded the meditation I felt my heart begin to lighten.

I was shocked at the end of the meditation. I looked at my phone: my partner, whom I'd had an argument with that morning, had texted me to apologise. A girlfriend I had not spoken to for a long time reached out for a coffee. My sisters texted me to let me know they wanted to have dinner the following week. My mentor sent me a text to check in with me. In 20 minutes I had shifted my mental state to gratitude and forgiveness and took total responsibility for the relationships in my life. The result was that these relationships showed up in my life as only love. It felt like a miracle, a miracle I had created.

This is a radical theory, but some of the most radical theories hold the greatest gifts for us. To become courageous we are going to have to be radical at times in our forgiving; our healing depends on this. Ultimately, our healing leads to emotional freedom, which gives us more energy to move forward powerfully in life. To move forward on the Courageous Path and with velocity we must assume total responsibility for our relationships; we can step into forgiveness through the powerful mantra of the Ho'oponopono prayer.

KATHARINE AND ISABEL: FORGET TRYING TO LEAVE A LEGACY

Someone is sitting in the shade today, because someone planted a tree a long time ago.

WARREN BUFFETT

Trying to leave a legacy is hard work on the Courageous Path. We can become obsessed with leaving something behind and ask: what is my legacy? Is this my legacy? Is it good enough? This focus takes us away from the present moment, yet it is in the present moment that the legacy is created without effort, just presence. When we focus too much on the future, not only does the present moment disappear but the legacy we so wish for is diluted or disappears. The author of *Grounded Spirituality*, Jeff Brown, wrote: 'Deepening into the moment reveals your purpose, while deepening into your purpose expands your presence.'

Isabel and her mother Katharine were very close, sharing a massive passion for studying people, their personalities, their quirks and their motivations. Both were fiction writers who knew that to write great fiction they needed to understand what made people tick and behave in certain ways. They were two amateur peas in a psychology pod.

One day Isabel met a dashing man, Clarence, whom she fell quickly and madly in love with. Unfortunately Katharine, who was a little obsessed with finding a perfect match for her daughter, wasn't a fan of Clarence (yikes!). She did not think they were compatible at all. Isabel was bookish, academic and an intensely feeling woman, while Clarence was just a little too logical, a man of few words, a strong, silent type. Katharine also felt he was a bit of a misfit among their family. Katharine did not want to lose her loving bond with her only daughter – marriage can sometimes do that – so she was determined to deepen her understanding of Clarence's personality.

Katharine would call her psychologist friend Carl Jung (yes, that Carl) and have long rambling chats about different personalities. Initially, Katharine focused on Clarence, but soon found herself studying many others: adults, children and anyone who stopped by to visit her home. She shared her observations and theories with her daughter, who listened and absorbed everything.

Over time Clarence and Isabel had their own children, and as their children grew up Isabel wanted new meaning in her life. She came across the Humm-Wadsworth Temperament Scale, a psychological test designed to help place people in the right jobs. This was right up her alley, as she had been studying this stuff with her mother her *whole* life. She started working for the man who developed the scale, but despite her optimism the job disappointed her. Isabel came to see that the scale was not a useful measure at all, and found that employees were not being correctly matched to jobs that suited them. Isabel quit her job and contacted her mum immediately. She proposed that together they come up with a new assessment to help people understand themselves.

It is hard to say if Isabel and Katharine were born in the wrong or right era. If they were born now hands down they would have thrived with a sisterhood around them, but they were born in the Victorian era, where there were no expectations for women other than to birth and raise children. Perhaps this was the key to their legacy. They were early female pioneers with a strong desire to help people know themselves, so first they started analysing themselves and each other, then their husbands and kids. It grew organically. They were not held back by their lack of formal training in psychology and were not conditioned by the rigour of the rules of testing scientific theories. They got dirty and tried new things. They were not afraid to fail. They made up their own processes. They took their time. They were not in a rush because they had nothing to prove and no legacy to try and leave. They were just being themselves.

Isabel Briggs and Katharine Myers would years later change the world with their Myers-Briggs personality test, a questionnaire indicating differing psychological preferences in how people perceive the world and make decisions. In her biography, Isabel Briggs Myers wrote that one of the principles she lived by was freedom: 'To work at what interests me most, with minimum expenditure of time and energy on non-essentials.' Many of us know our four Myers-Briggs letters, and it is a test that has stood the test of time. Did Katharine and Isabel try to create a legacy? No. They followed their passions and curiosity and did not let anyone distract them. Inevitably, their legacy was created.

Your presence will create the legacy so just focus on the present moment.

PIP: COURAGEOUS SELF-BELIEF

I always believed that I could make it, or I would never have spent so many years trying to get there.

HELEN REDDY

When you put your self-worth in the hands of others you rely on their judgement, then you exhaust yourself seeking it and in the process your self-belief is eroded.

We don't think of resignation letters to our employers as love letters, yet my resignation as an executive director from the corporate world was a love letter to myself. How often do we stay in situations that stop serving us? This isn't just about jobs, but about relationships, marriages and leaky apartments. Sometimes walking away is a great act of self-love.

Things hadn't gone south at work; it was just that I was starting to love my intuitive work more. I knew it was time to step up as a spiritual teacher and work full time as a medium. My life didn't make sense if I didn't do this work. My transition between two worlds was over, and I felt the pull to make a greater commitment to my life path. I knew the next step forward I needed to take and I wanted to talk about it with a friend. Perhaps I wanted to hear the conviction in my own voice.

I called my friend, Pip Drysdale. You may recall Pip is an author and more importantly someone I looked up to who embodied the absolute act of courage. During one of our regular chats I asked: 'What does it mean to be courageous?' She'd been writing even when there was no book deal in sight. Writing was something she had done in different forms for years and she knew this was what she wanted to do with her life. No external validation needed.

Her answer? 'Well, once you realise that not doing something is a bigger risk than doing it, courage comes easily.'

Do you have consistent thoughts telling you what to do with your life?
How can you act on these thoughts?

'So did the self-belief come after you got the book deal?' I asked. I was questioning what type of validation I would need to start feeling successful in my new career path. I was beginning to understand that perhaps validation was not the solution. What validation could people even give me?

'Don't get me wrong: it felt amazing when I got the book deal. I remember being incredibly anxious waiting for months to hear back from you guys [at the time I was working for the publisher that would sign her, that's how we met]. By the same token, because of all the work that went into making the book good at that point – the rewrites and rewrites – it also felt like the logical next step. There were just so many small steps along the way. On one hand I was so grateful and I felt so lucky. On the other hand it felt like the obvious next step.'

Self-belief builds with many courageous steps forward.
You stop needing validation.

At some point in life we stop needing validation. We stop needing to prove ourselves and we start to move in flow with the natural transitions. I had studied countless spiritual texts and had attended a mountain of esoteric workshops and many public appearances, including live psychic and mediumship readings on television and in front of a live audience. I started to feel that stepping away from my corporate role completely was the natural next step for me. I did have self-belief, but I needed reminding. The version of myself that constantly doubted had faded into the background. I was serving clients. It actually didn't feel like a leap any more; it felt like the next logical step. But my mind needed to see it this way. I realised that if I believed I could or couldn't then either way I was right. So why not believe that I could?

I thought that when Simon & Schuster offered Pip the book deal she had reached some mountain peak, but *she* believed in her work and *she* believed she would be published. She believed in her writing. The many powerful steps and long hours spent honing her craft had formed a coating of self-belief. Truthfully, after all the work she had put in, if the publishing house I had worked for had not offered her a deal someone else would have, or she would have self-published. Her self-belief in her work was all she needed. The external validation was a mirror of her own internal validation.

By the act of following your dreams you have already succeeded.

After that conversation with Pip I typed my resignation letter. It was only when I let out a deep long exhale at the end of typing the letter that I realised I had just typed a goodbye letter to the life I had come to know and identify with. At this point on my Courageous Path, ignoring the signs to do the spiritual work full time felt ominous. I had been through many dark nights of courage and now I was equipped with foresight that had taught me to move forward empowered. Empowered doesn't always mean comfortable or easy, but I was in action and I was ready and willing to take more powerful steps forward.

I was saying goodbye to my executive salary, my sparkly title, my social standing within my family, my status. But as I typed this short and direct letter I knew I was telling my higher self 'I am choosing you now.' I was telling my intuition 'I am listening to you, really listening.' I was telling the universe 'I surrender, please help me out. Please, universe, start working things out behind the scenes so I am not left penniless.' I was also powerfully telling family and friends 'I am stepping forward. Come with me on this path. If you can't, that is okay. I will go it alone.'

It was a different kind of Courageous Leap moment. I was filled with greater self-belief, a knowing it would be all right and a knowing it would be challenging again. The dark nights were not over, but I was better equipped to deal with them.

Self-belief is the product of perseverance to do the things you are meant to do with your life.

COURAGEOUS TRUTHS

1. Saying yes before you are ready is an act of courage.
2. There are times on the Courageous Path where focus, action, diligence and hard work will be required. It will feel like you are running a marathon. You've got this!
3. Don't quit until you realise your dreams. Then you will be called to dream another dream.
4. Be unreasonable in your requests and you will be unreasonably rewarded.

5. The Hoʻoponopono prayer is a powerful mantra to assist you to step into forgiveness and to heal relationships.
6. Your passion will create your legacy.
7. Self-belief builds with many small courageous steps.

GET CURIOUS QUESTIONS

1. When was the last time you said yes to something you were scared to do? How did it turn out?
2. Where has hard work already paid off in your life or in the life of someone you admire?
3. Who has role modelled to you the rewards of hard work?
4. When you feel like quitting, who in your soul tribe will you call?
5. Where can you be more unreasonable in your requests in service of your purpose?

POWER PHRASE

'I am capable of doing the hard things with ease and grace.'

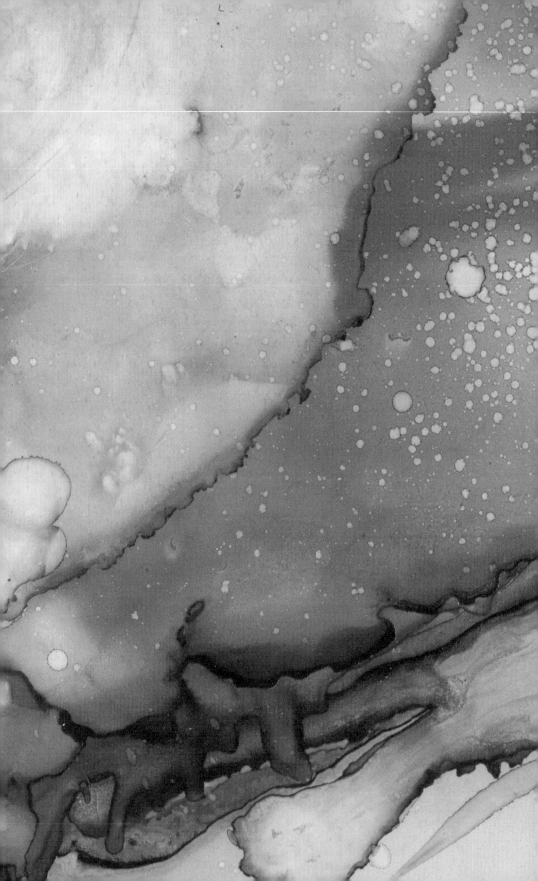

CHAPTER 14

Courageous cycles

We have been poisoned by fairy tales.

– ANAÏS NIN

AFTER THE FAIRY TALE ENDS

Life is not a fairy tale, nor is it a tragedy.

I am sitting with a cast of five little people under the age of seven: my nephews and niece. It is storytelling time and I am modernising and recreating a continuation of their beloved fairy tales. They are all ears. These little ones dislike it when the story ends; I think adults are the same. When a chapter ends in our life we do seek out the next one to follow. On our Courageous Paths we are always seeking growth and new experiences.

What becomes of Cinderella? I mean, what happens after she marries Prince Charming? Is it happily ever after? She wants financial independence and has always thought there was a greater meaning to her life, otherwise what was the point of the difficulties she faced? After her wedding she takes off her glass slippers and grounds her vision into reality. This is her Courageous Path. She starts an online shoe business to help disadvantaged women in faraway kingdoms who don't have shoes. Her marriage goes through a rough patch as she travels a lot, but she and the prince get through it with counselling and commitment. They create a household where chores are split and finances are shared. As a busy double income, no kids household, Cinderella and Prince Charming make every moment together count. They both have a life purpose and are committed to their marriage. It takes work that they are both prepared to do.

Do you remember the three little pigs? A decade later the pigs lose their house due to a financial crisis; however, they are resourceful. They crowd fund and build a successful wealth-coaching business called Claim Your Inner Swine: Sow Your Seeds of Wealth. They are now a Fortune 100 company. After being interviewed by well-known wealth creator Robert Kiyosaki they become famous. They give 10 per cent of their profits to the Vegan Institute of America. They don't just speak about financial literacy, but also about resilience and mindset. The three of them are a soul tribe. They thought facing the wolf was courageous, but really being seen in a world that did not value little pigs or their voices took the most courage.

Finally, what happened to Snow White and the seven dwarfs? It didn't actually work out with Prince Charming because Snow White had a lot of inherited fear-based beliefs she had not worked through. Anxiously attached to love, she got married a little too quickly and, after a short while, she and Prince Charming divorced. She dates a lot of men, but none of those relationships work either. A fairy godmother mentor comes along her path and she starts to do the big inner work. She realises that her stepmother's own mother was cruel to her during her childhood and Snow White comes to terms with being abandoned by both her mother and stepmother. She realises they triggered each other so much when they spent time together. Snow White pilgrimages to foreign lands and mothers herself during this process. It takes time. In her late 40s she decides to start running mother and daughter healing retreats. The seven dwarfs are all involved: social media, publicity, events, production. They stood by her through the entire process. The work never stops for all of them, but they are all enrolled in the larger cause. They have all found meaning and purpose in their childhood challenges.

Life isn't a fairy tale, and life is not meant to be an unlived, uninspired or inauthentic experience. Social media and wearing rose-coloured glasses can betray our reality. The Courageous Path continues the expansion of ourselves and our relationships. The work never ends, but why would it? By continuing to walk on this path we love and are loved more deeply.

REALITY BITES

Courage doesn't always roar. Sometimes courage is the little voice at the end of the day that says I'll try again tomorrow.

MARY ANNE RADMACHER

We think the tests in life are over when we have scaled up and climbed over tall walls, but really we have built up fortitude and strong muscles that will help us face the next wall. The tests keep on coming at the most unexpected moments; this is how we continue to grow on the Courageous Path.

I know this from my own experience of stepping into my purpose as a medium and spiritual teacher. I am now a woman who has learned how to give and receive love in balance and to honour my own Courageous Path in a way that makes sense to only myself. Little did I understand the twists and turns, Courageous Leaps required and signs received, dark nights and soul tribe help I would experience on my path to writing this book. I know I have a further distance to walk on my Courageous Path, more walls to scale and greater terrain ahead of me.

KATE: THE YOGA STUDIO OPENING

Barn's burnt down – now I can see the moon.

MIZUTA MASAHIDE

Do you remember Kate, who handed in her police badge to walk the path of the yogi?

I was invited to the grand opening of Kate's yoga studio, which had required three solid months of work to get to this point. You could still faintly smell the fresh paint job her husband had worked so hard to finish. The grand opening was a huge success. Kate had created a new life for herself; new yogi friends, clients and a local community all gathered around. I watched her beaming with excitement and pride. She couldn't believe how much she had managed to do.

Kate had run a marathon to get to the opening night, but the marathon was still not over. Her husband, the one person she wanted to share the moment with, wasn't able to make the special occasion. He had been diagnosed with bowel cancer and had been operated on to remove a tumour just a couple of days earlier.

She confided to me at the end of the evening: 'He was heavily sedated so we couldn't speak on the phone either.'

The Courageous Path continues to test us. This is the way we continually grow and expand.

Kate's husband made a full recovery from his cancer treatment. Kate's yoga studio is thriving. She took another leap and applied to create a health and wellness expo in her local community. She knows how to say yes to offers from the universe before she is ready. Kate has achieved some significant gluten-free brownie points stepping forward on her Courageous Path. But not only that, she inspired her four children by being courageous. She has shown them the importance of self-love and authenticity. She was courageous for her husband, who was there with her along the way as he was fighting cancer. Kate has learned that life is both messy and magical at the same time.

On the Courageous Path miracles happen and we are also touched by tragedy. In between we are swept along by the mundane and the monotony of responsibility. The ending is never the ending, just a beginning to a new cycle. We must be courageous enough to surrender to the endings and to honour the beginnings.

TIFFANY: YOU MUST BOTH BE READY

One child, one teacher, one book, one pen can change the world.
MALALA YOUSAFZAI

Sometimes we walk the Courageous Path as a large collective group. The 2020 COVID-19 pandemic propelled millions of people onto their Courageous Paths. Some voluntarily stepped forward, some were pushed and many resisted. Unnecessary routines in our lives were banished, our greedy consumption declined, our creativity was boosted. We got to take one long, much-needed exhale. The brave took the opportunity to take a good, long, hard look at every aspect of their lives. It was extremely uncomfortable, incredibly difficult, excruciating at times and ultimately necessary. This was the courageous work that many of us had been delaying for a long time. Truthfully, there was no time to do this reflective work previously. We were busy working hard, on long commutes and glued to social media.

According to Spotify, Podcast listening doubled during the early months of the pandemic. Around that time Tiffany, who founded Sister Suppers, was thinking to relaunch a podcast series she had begun two years before. Her podcast is called Conversation with Tee-Ta and Tiffany: A Black Girl and a White Girl Talking. The purpose of the podcast is to assist women who do not know how to move forward with conversations and understanding around race relations, with a greater vision to abolish racism, inequalities and biased behaviours in America.

Timing is everything. You can't rush your Courageous Path and you can't slow down either. Global and community influences will shape you. You must be responsive, adaptable and brave. Two years prior, Tiffany hadn't been ready to completely embody her vision and voice; the world hadn't been ready either. Then, on 25 May 2020, George Floyd's death in custody in the US ignited the worldwide Black Lives Matter movement. This was the next step we were being called on to make on the collective Courageous Path. COVID-19 had been the great equaliser, and Floyd's death and the ensuing protests showed us that we could not run from the bigger question of race inequality. The world was now ready for Tiffany's podcast.

I spoke with Tiffany in July 2020. She talked about what changed for her in those two years: 'I spent two years really understanding the black culture, the white culture and not just in the US but in Australia too. I ended up with a black boyfriend. The impact of George Floyd touched me on a new level because that could have happened to my boyfriend.'

I asked Tiffany: 'Were you scared speaking out about such a sensitive topic and in a country that was not your own?' As a dark-skinned woman living in a culture I was born into that was not my own, I knew that speaking out required courage.

'Definitely! I thought: I am going to look stupid and people are going to judge me. Then I also thought: if I need to be the stupid white girl asking the stupid questions and that helps other people to wake up and do the same and to speak out when injustice happens, well, I am okay to be that person.'

Tiffany had the courage to follow her purpose and, as a self-proclaimed movement maker, knew how to bring people on the journey with her for a common cause. 'Every time one person reaches out after listening to my podcast and says "This has changed me", that's enough to keep me going.'

On the Courageous Path you will be called to stand for a human or animal right, to stand up against injustices and to heal the world and your community. You now realise the importance you have in creating a new world for the next generation. You also realise you have the power to do this. Check out #ablackgirlawhitegirl and become a follower.

KATH: LETTING LOVE IN

A career is wonderful, but you can't curl up with it on a cold night.
MARILYN MONROE

Remember Kath who busked on the London Underground and then ended up directing and producing a musical on the West End? She called me out of the blue. 'I have just picked up a part-time role at Bumble to earn some extra income.' Bumble is a dating app with the philosophy that 'when members of the opposite sex match on Bumble, women are required to make the first move'. It is modern dating at its best.

'I am the interim hive keeper. It is the fancy title they give the office manager. I really love it. And guess what: I love this company so much I am actually thinking of giving online dating a go.'

Stop press! This was a revolutionary statement: Kath had been firmly against online dating. It was an absolute no-go zone regardless of how many times I insisted she needed to get out there and start dating. It was always a curtain call on discussing this subject.

'I just feel so ready to meet someone now. I have focused on my career for so long that I now realise love is something I have overlooked.' Arriving at this destination in her career gave Kath a new perspective. 'Making it to the place I wanted to be in within my career has actually highlighted what is missing from other parts of my life: being in a loving romantic relationship.'

Sometimes when we work hard in one aspect of life we forgo another aspect of life. It is easy to do when our calling firmly beckons us.

Kath was in a new cycle of her Courageous Path. She would be called to make leaps of courage and say yes before she was ready. She had spent time learning self-love. The Courageous Path took her on a journey to honouring her dreams and now courage was helping her to honour her heart. She later said that it took even more courage to go on a blind date than it did to audition for a West End musical.

The Courageous Path will always call us to look at *all* aspects of our life. A courageously lived life is a life lived with an open heart to both receiving and giving love.

NATALIE: LOSING THE TITLES

Happiness is a form of courage.

HOLBROOK JACKSON

Natalie Faber-Castell is a countess, a title of nobility that is a birthright for her. Natalie has shed the title she was born into, along with the conventional titles she had acquired during her life: wife, marketing director, honours graduate. These titles are squeaky clean, relatable and easy to understand. When you are a free spirit a title can feel like a weighty burden. Like masks, titles are things we can hide behind.

The titles Natalie now wears with pride are divorced supermum, sound healer, energy coach, meditation teacher, workshop facilitator, voice coach, song writer and volunteer. I call her Wonder Woman every time we meet for coffee.

'I have completely given up fitting in and living up to other people's expectations.'

For Natalie, the Courageous Path was an unwinding and unravelling road. 'I feel like I have gone back to the beginning, right before I got married where I had just graduated from Princeton University with an Honours in musical composition. And I have just gotten off a zoom call where I have facilitated a song writing workshop for fifteen incredibly talented teenagers. I forgot what this felt like.'

I could feel Natalie's buzzing energy through the phone call.

Sometimes our Courageous Path can be a road where we walk back to the beginning to remember what we loved and then walk forward on our own terms and conditions. And sometimes we need to shed all the titles we have picked up along the way to allow for this to happen.

THE PATH FORWARD

Courage is the most important of all the virtues because without courage one cannot practice any virtues consistently.

MAYA ANGELOU

At the beginning of your Courageous Path you might have thought the path would answer your calling, fulfil your dharma and help you step into your purpose. And yes, it can, but you now realise it is so much more than that. The Courageous Path is the path of living your life authentically and truthfully. When you are courageous you allow the path to shape, remould and unravel you. It is the journey you seek and not the destination. This is the adventure you signed up to and for a while you forgot, but now you have remembered.

The Courageous Path is not linear; it is a cycle that spirals upwards. The upwards motion relates to your expanded courage, insights, wisdom and resilience. You grow with each cycle. There is no prescribed length of time to walk the path.

We are all walking a path in life, but is it a Courageous Path? Having come this far through to the final chapter you will now realise that the first step on the Courageous Path is making a commitment to change and accepting and understanding that the status quo is no longer working. You know this takes a daring and awakened mindset. It also takes an awareness of the pain you are in and an acknowledgement that your life will only change when you commit to making inner changes. You understand that you may have suppressed your intuition, betrayed your dreams, denied your feminine nature and loved others too hard and yourself too little. You are ready to ask yourself the Dangerous Questions: dangerous because they will call for an honest response. You are ready to answer them.

You understand that your purpose is found in the wisdom gleaned from the tragedies and challenges of your life, your unlived childhood dreams. You search for a life of meaning and appreciate this involves being of service to the world. You start to connect the dots in your life and now your life events and experiences start to make sense.

You know and believe that the universe is guiding you. You are no longer shocked when you receive a sign from the universe. You are grateful and are worthy of receiving a sign that points to your purpose, your destiny, the next right turn.

You have mastered your Courageous Leaps, one of the first great initiations on the Courageous Path. You understand that fear will be present, but so will excitement. The Courageous Leap is a rite of passage to claiming yourself and your identity: the lost you. You know that in embracing the courage to leap you will land where you are meant to.

When you land you will meet others who have taken their leaps of courage. Soul sisters, soul mothers and soul mentors will appear. You know that courage is a magnet for support and connection.

The Courageous Path is the path of awakening permanently. This is catalysed by your Dark Night of Courage. The acuteness of the pain is largely forgotten; the transformation is what remains. The course correction has happened. Your life looks different after the dark night and it is meant to. You have grown to be spiritually courageous and may feel super human. This is the real education you have been seeking. You have faith in the universe, you meditate, you journal, you breathe deeply. You also swear, laugh and rest when you need to. You are in a state of flow and always connected to the universe that guides you and surprises you.

When you take detours off your Courageous Path you are bumped back in line. Your perfectionist self will rear her head. She is the unloved child you need to tend to, to support, love and guide. When you fail you learn and a new wiser cycle begins.

You have healed the big misunderstood wounds in your life. This is the most challenging and transformational part of the path. Again, you are supported by your soul tribe and the universe as you do this work.

At times you will need to be in big action on the path and it will feel like a marathon, and you now know you have the stamina. You are ready to trust that it is okay to say yes even before you feel ready. It is uncomfortable, but you know the rewards on the other side. Courage is the most solid foundation you can build your life on.

You are now becoming a teacher and way shower. You have the lived experience of being courageous. You are starting to show others how to do this. They seek you out. The Courageous Path was your initiation to show them the way to be courageously themselves.

For all of us the cycles will repeat. Now you are ready to take new courageous steps onto new Courageous Paths and be courageously you.

COURAGEOUS TRUTHS

1. Life is not a fairy tale, nor is it a tragedy. The Courageous Path is a continual expansion of yourself and your relationships. It is a never-ending journey.
2. Expect the tests to keep on coming, perhaps at the most unexpected moments. This is how you continue to grow on the Courageous Path.
3. You may be called to find your vision and your voice again and again on the Courageous Path. At some point you will be ready and so will the world.
4. The Courageous Path will call you to look at *all* aspects of your life.
5. Sometimes you need to shed all the titles you have acquired through your life and take on new and authentic titles.
6. Once you have walked your Courageous Path you will inspire, mentor and lead others to walk theirs.

GET CURIOUS QUESTIONS

1. When you now reflect back on your Courageous Path so far, what are your proudest moments?
2. Who do you already lead, mentor and inspire? Who might you lead, mentor and inspire in the future?
3. Describe the courageous and brave things you have already done on your path so far.
4. It is 12 months from now: describe the brave and courageous things you did that you are now celebrating.

POWER PHRASE

'I am courageously me and I inspire others.'

Walk the Courageous Path with me

GET ON THE LIST

Receive free teachings and gifts by signing up for my newsletter at www.sheilav/signup.

GET STUFF FOR FREE

I love empowering women as they walk on their Courageous Path. Check out the link www.sheilav.co/free-gifts for free resources that will support you on your path.

ONLINE COURSES

If you like this book and want to go deeper check out my online courses, events and retreats in your city; go to www.sheilav.co.

STAY IN TOUCH

Stay in touch with me through:

- www.sheilav.co
- Facebook: SheilaVempoweringintuition
- Joining my closed Facebook group to be supported in brave conversations by your soul tribe: thecourageouspath
- Instagram: sheila_v__

Bibliography

Alcoholics Anonymous. *Pass It on: The Story of Bill Wilson and How the A.A. Message Reached the World*, Alcoholics Anonymous World Service Inc., 1984.

Baron-Reid, Colette. 'The Cledon: How to Get More Powerful Divine Guidance in Your Everyday Life!', www.colettebaronreid.com, https://www.colettebaronreid.com/2010/03/08/the-cledon-how-to-get-more-powerful-divine-guidance-in-your-everyday-life/

Bialylew, Elise. *The Happiness Plan*, Affirm, 2018.

Brown, Brené. *Braving the Wilderness: The Quest for True Belonging and the Courage to Stand Alone*, Random House, 2017.

Brown, Jeff. *Grounded Spirituality*, Enrealment Press, 2019.

Cameron, Julia. *The Artist's Way*, Pan Macmillan UK, 2016.

Duhigg, Charles. *The Power of Habit: Why we do what we do and how to change*, Random House UK, 2013.

Friends in Recovery. *12 Steps: A Way Out: A Spiritual Process for Healing*, Recovery Publications Inc., 2012.

Hay, Louise L. *You Can Heal Your Life*, Hay House, 1985.

Helliwell, J.F. et al. (eds). *2020 World Happiness Report*, Sustainable Development Solutions Network, 2020

Huffington, Arianna. *Thrive*, Random House UK, 2015.

'It's a Three-Peat, Finland Keeps Top Spot as Happiest Country in World', *World Happiness Report 2020*, 20 March 2020, https://worldhappiness.report/news/its-a-three-peat-finland-keeps-top-spot-as-happiest-country-in-world/.

Kabat-Zinn, Jon. *Wherever You Go, There You Are: Mindfulness Meditation for Everyday Life*, Little Brown, 2004.

Murdoch, Maureen. *The Heroine's Journey*, Random House US, 1990.

Myers, Isabel Briggs and Myers, Peter B. *Gifts Differing: Understanding Personality Type*, John Murray Press, 2010.

Myss, Caroline. 'The Three Stages of Self Esteem', www.myss.com, https://www.myss.com/cmed/online-institute/series/the-three-stages-of-self-esteem/.

Noontil, Annette. *The Body is the Barometer of the Soul: So be Your Own Doctor II*, Lucienne Noontil, 1994.

Norwood, Robin. *Women Who Love Too Much*, Simon & Schuster US, 2008.

Nylund, Joanna. *The Finnish Art of Courage*, Octopus, 2018.

Pinkola Estes, Clarissa. *Women Who Run With the Wolves*, Random House UK, 2008.

Porter, Jon. 'Spotify podcast consumption doubles as overall listening recovers', *The Verge*, 29 July 2020. https://www.theverge.com/2020/7/29/21346339/spotify-q2-2020-earnings-podcasts-coronavirus-covid-19-consumption-recovery.

Schucman, Helen. *A Course in Miracles*, Foundation For Inner Peace, Combined Volume (3rd edition) 2008.

Shapiro, Shauna. 'The Power of Mindfulness: What You Practice Grows Stronger', Tedx Washington Square, 10 March 2017, https://www.youtube.com/watch?v=IeblJdB2-Vo&list=RD0qGS3IL772c.

Shapiro, Shauna. *Good Morning, I Love You: Mindfulness + Self-Compassion Practices to Rewire Your Brain for Calm, Clarity + Joy*, St Martins Press, 2020.

Sivers, Derek. 'How To Start A Movement', TED Ideas Worth Spreading, https://www.ted.com/talks/derek_sivers_how_to_start_a_movement?language=en.

Sogyal Rinpoche. *The Tibetan Book of Living and Dying*, Random House UK, 2017.

Stevenson, Jane and Kaplan, Dan. 'Women C-Suite Ranks Nudge Up—a Tad', www.kornferry.com. https://www.kornferry.com/insights/articles/women-in-leadership-2019-statistics.

Tolle, Eckhart. *The Power of Now: A Guide to Spiritual Enlightenment*, New World Library, 2004.

Trent, Tererai. *The Awakened Woman*, Atria/Enliven Books, 2018.

University of California, Los Angeles. 'UCLA Researchers Identify Key Biobehavioral Pattern Used By Women To Manage Stress', *Science Daily,* 22 May 2000, bit.ly/ 3nXe8cy.

Velázquez, Marta. 'Sisu: Beyond Perseverance', *Positive Psychology News,* 15 December 2014. https://positivepsychologynews.com/news/marta-velazquez/2014121530618.

Vitale, Joe and Len, Ihaleakala Hew. *Zero Limits: The Secret Hawaiian System for Wealth, Health, Peace, and More,* John Wiley & Sons Inc., 2008.

Ware, Bronnie. *The Top Five Regrets of the Dying: Life Transformed by the Dearly Departing,* Hay House, 2019.

Webster, Bethany. 'Mother Wound Healing: Why It's Crucial For Women', www.bethanywebster.com, https://www.bethanywebster.com/mother-wound-healing/.

Acknowledgements

The greatest and most fulfilling accomplishments in life are done with a wonderful team around you. This book has been no exception.

Thank you to my family: my mother (for teaching me that brave is about living greatly the life that is offered to us), my father (for teaching me that brave is a life of no regrets), Vaneeta (for showing me how to generously mother) and Ramona (for showing me how to serve a cause greater than myself). .

Thank you brave Samuel McLennan, my bearded soulmate, for having my front and back in life, for your love, support and big courageous heart. Thank you for the fun adventures as we walk side by side, holding hands, on our Courageous Paths.

Thank you to the delicious chocolate Tim Tams in my life for your enduring friendship, love and support. To Darlean Williams (for your commitment as a true best friend), Alex Thompson (for your grounded wisdom), Toni Borthwick (for the constant laughs), Cindy Gudykunst (for being a wise fashionista oracle), Tiffany Scott (for showing me how to be a stand for change), Kath Haling (for being a next-level-awesome human), Pip Drysdale (for inspiring me to be a better writer), Van Le (for allowing me to truly lean on you; you are a pillar of strength), Andrew Flannery (for the sage quotes), Andrés Engracia (for your Merlin advice), Lisa Martin (for showing me what friendship means), Peter Hoare (for always being a phone call away), Vivienne Somers (for your sassiness, grit and immense astrology wisdom), Ellyn Shander (for your unconditional love), Tammi Kirkness (way shower manifestor extraordinaire) and Jai Coucil (for your hysterical astrology counselling).

Louise Winchester, this book and the next chapter of my life would not have happened without you. Thank you for the nudge and sometimes the much-needed push forward. You are an inspiring spiritual teacher.

To my wise soul mentors, thank you for your generosity in sharing your wisdom: Avril Norman, Daniella Divine, Pauline Nguyen, Rebecca Mayhew, Rebekah Fisher and Tom Cronin.

A full life has been filled with truly inspiring, generous and talented people, and my life is richer for knowing you: Adrian Kaleel, Ange Teulon, Asha George,

Bella Zanesco, Bella Laquarta, Celeste Moroney, Caroline Bonpain, Christine Morgan, Chris Drew, Dadhichi Toth, Dan Ruffino, Derrin Brown, Debbie Tennant, Elissa Baille, Jemma Birrell, Jov Jitsu, Joanne Raso, Janelle Zammit, Lee Williams, Lara Ellis, Karen Bowie, Maggie Hamilton, Margot Saville, Melissa Legge, Michelle LaForest, Michael Muir, Peter Bliss, Poppy Spinos, River and Sali, Sommer, Susan Kemsley, Susan Rudd, Susanne Rauer, Tee Cooper, Janelle Campbell, Louisa Seton, Raewyn Tierney, Jess Pearson and Trish Haywood.

It takes a village to create a book, so thank you to the incredible Rockpool Publishing team. Lisa Hanrahan, Paul Dennett and Sara Lindberg: thank you for your shared vision, hard work and dedication.

Laurel Cohn (I am forever indebted to your incredible editing prowess! Thank you for holding my hand tightly from the beginning to the end), Zena Shapter and Tricia Dearborn (for weaving your wordsmith magic throughout these pages).

My heart explodes with gratitude for the brave women and men who leant their voices to this book to inspire and heal the feminine. I bow my head in reverence for the brave lives you have lived and the generosity of your heart to share your stories. Thank you to Alice Cheng, Amy Oscar, Angie Cowen, Barbara Brangan, Carol McGregor, Ellyn Shander, Jovina Rasiah, Kate Karpanko, Kath Haling, Leon Nacson, Lisa Clark, Melinda Rushe, Natalie Grace, Pip Drysdale, Ruby Lohman, Dr Shauna Shapiro, Tiffany Scott, Van Le and Vivienne Somers.

I stand on the broad shoulders of many light workers, authors, soul mentors, visionaries, thought leaders, psychologists, yogis and spiritual teachers. Thank you for your words both spoken and written. Your wisdom and your Courageous Paths showed me how to walk my own.

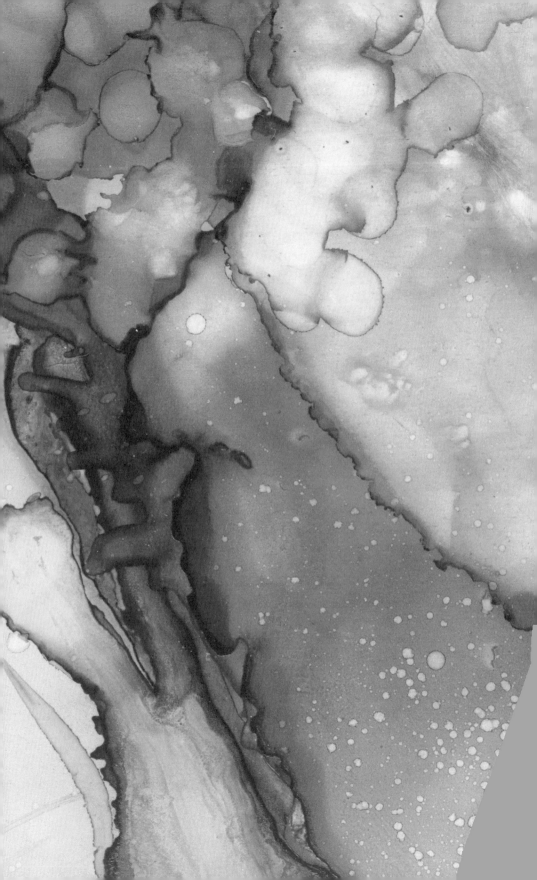

About the Author

Sheila has mastered the art of blending two diametrically opposite careers: she is a corporate leader as well as a spiritual teacher and mentor, medium and psychic reader. She holds an MBA and has fifteen years' experience in publishing and media preceded by a foundation of eight years' experience in chartered accounting and banking. She was also the CFO of a global publishing company.

Sheila is the founder of Empowering Intuition. Her natural mediumistic and psychic abilities were passed down through multiple generations in her family, and she cultivated those skills at the prestigious Arthur Findlay College. She immersed herself in learning reiki and multiple mindfulness techniques at Esalen with Dr Shauna Shapiro, and studied bhakti yoga and the Vedic teachings of Kripalu Maharaj. She was taught by world-renowned medium James Van Praagh at The Omega Institute and studied executive coaching and NLP with Tad James Co. She appeared on Australian television on Psychic TV. Sheila combines corporate smarts with her deep intuition to provide grounded practical advice in her sessions.

WWW.SHEILAV.CO